# SHEPHERD'S NOTES

D1566926

# SHEPHERD'S NOTES

## *Christian Classics*

# *C. S. Lewis's Miracles*

BROADMAN
&HOLMAN
PUBLISHERS

Nashville, Tennessee

Shepherd's Notes—C. S. Lewis *Miracles*
© 2000
by Broadman & Holman Publishers
Nashville, Tennessee
All rights reserved
Printed in the United States of America

0–8054–9394–8
Dewey Decimal Classification: 231.73
Subject Heading: C. S. Lewis
Library of Congress Card Catalog Number: 99–37901

**Dedicated to Nicole Miethe,
with a father's love for his daughter**

**Library of Congress Cataloging-in-Publication Data**
Miethe, Terry L., 1948–
    C. S. Lewis' Miracles / by Terry L. Miethe.
        p.  cm.  — (Shepherd's notes. Christian classics)
    Includes bibliographical references.
    ISBN 0–8054–9394–8 (alk. paper)
    1. Lewis, C. S. (Clive Staples), 1898–1963. Miracles.  2. Miracles.  I. Title.
II. Series.
BT97.M45   1999
231.7'3—dc21                                                                    99–37901
                                                                                        CIP

1 2 3 4 5 6   03 02 01 00
R

# CONTENTS

Dear Reader:

*Shepherd's Notes—Classics Series* is designed to give you a quick, step-by-step overview of some of the enduring treasures of the Christian faith. They are designed to be used alongside the classic itself—either in individual study or in a study group.

Classics have staying power. Although they were written in a particular place and time and often in response to situations different than our own, they deal with problems, concerns, and themes that transcend time and place.

The faithful of all generations have found spiritual nourishment in the Scriptures and in the works of Christians from earlier generations. Martin Luther and John Calvin would not have become who they were apart from their reading Augustine. God used the writings of Martin Luther to move John Wesley from a religion of dead works to an experience at Aldersgate in which his "heart was strangely warmed."

It is an awesome sight—these streams of gracious influence flowing from generation to generation.

*Shepherd's Notes—Classics Series* will help you take the first steps in claiming and drawing strength from your spiritual heritage.

*Shepherd's Notes* is designed to bridge the gap between now and then and to help you understand, love, and benefit from the company of saints of an earlier time. Each volume gives you an overview of the main themes dealt with by the author and then walks with you step-by-step through the classic.

Enjoy!
In Him,

David R. Shepherd
Editor-in-Chief

## DESIGNED FOR THE BUSY USER

*Shepherd's Notes* for Lewis's *Miracles* is designed to provide an easy-to-use tool for gaining a quick overview of the major themes and the structure of *Miracles*.

*Shepherd's Notes* are designed for laymen, pastors, teachers, small-group leaders and participants, as well as the classroom student.

## DESIGNED FOR QUICK ACCESS

Persons with time restraints will especially appreciate the timesaving features built into *Shepherd's Notes*. All features are designed to work together to aid a quick and profitable encounter with *Miracles*—to point the reader to sections in *Miracles* where they may want to spend more time and go deeper.

*Chapter at a Glance*. Provides a listing of the major sections of the *Miracles*.

*Summary*. Each chapter of *Miracles* is summarized.

*Shepherd's Notes—Commentary*. Following the summary of the chapter, a commentary is provided. This enables the reader to look back and see the major themes that make up that particular chapter.

*Icons*. Various icons in the margin provide information to help the reader better understand that part of the text. Icons include:

*Shepherd's Notes Icon*. This icon denotes the commentary section of each chapter of the *Miracles*.

*Scripture Icon*. Scripture verses often illuminate passages in *Miracles*.

*Historical Background Icon*. Many passages in *Miracles* are better understood in the light of historical, cultural, biographical, and geographical information.

*Quotes Icon.* This icon marks significant quotes from *Miracles*.

*Points to Ponder Icon.* These questions and suggestions for further thought will be especially useful in helping both individuals and groups see the relevance of *Miracles* for our time.

# INTRODUCTION

Clive Staples Lewis, known the world over as C. S. Lewis, is the most famous defender of the Christian faith in the twentieth century. He was born in Belfast, Ireland, in 1898, the second son of Albert James Lewis and Flora Augusta Hamilton Lewis. Lewis talked about the emotional aspects of his family in *Surprised by Joy*, his spiritual autobiography up to 1931. His parents married in 1894. His brother Warren was born in 1895.

His father graduated from Lurgan College and became a solicitor—an attorney who advises clients and represents them in the lower courts. Albert Lewis was emotional and frequently unhappy. He was absorbed with politics. Clive disliked both the intense interest in politics and his emotional fluctuation. Lewis was indifferent to politics all his life, and his father's emotionalism left him apprehensive of outward exhibitions of feelings.

Lewis' mother graduated from Queen's College, Belfast, with a first-class degree in logic and a second-class in mathematics. She was happy and affectionate. She died in early August 1908 when Lewis was not yet ten years old.

Lewis spent two years, ages sixteen to eighteen, with W. T. Kirkpatrick as tutor, a well-known, if ruthless, teacher. Kirkpatrick wrote to Albert Lewis that Clive Staples could aspire to a career as a writer or a scholar but that he had little chance of succeeding at anything else. Whether the statement was true, it turned out to be almost prophetic. In the winter of 1916, Lewis went to Oxford to sit for entrance examinations

"If all the world were Christian, it might not matter if all the world were educated. But, as it is, a cultural life will exist outside the Church whether it exists inside or not. To be ignorant and simple now—not to be able to meet the enemies on their own ground—would be to throw down our weapons, and to betray our uneducated brethren who have, under God, no defense but us against the intellectual attacks of the heathen. Good philosophy must exist, if for no other reason, because bad philosophy needs to be answered"—C. S. Lewis, *The Weight of Glory and Other Addresses*.

1

The "rumor" is that Magdalen College, Cambridge, offered Lewis this professorship because he had been "snubbed" by Magdalen College, Oxford, and passed over time and again for a professorship because of colleagues' jealousy of the great success of his Christian writings. Thus, the college with the same name in Cambridge offered Lewis the professorship, in part, to put Oxford in its place.

and thus began a lifelong association with Oxford and Cambridge.

The first part of his Oxford degree was in Greek and Latin; the second, in philosophy. Because competition for teaching, or tutorial, positions was so fierce, Lewis was advised to take on a third area of study, so he read English language and literature. In one year he completed a three-year course, including learning Anglo- Saxon (Old English). Thus, he held three first-class degrees from Oxford. When he finally found a temporary appointment in philosophy, his first lecture was attended by only four students. In 1925, Lewis was awarded an English fellowship at Magdalen College, Oxford, where he stayed until January 1, 1955, when he went to Magdalen College, Cambridge, as professor of medieval and Renaissance literature. He held this position for seven and one-half years until July 1963, when he resigned because of poor health.

During World War II, Lewis became a champion of orthodox Christianity. He saw his "mission" as a defender in a spiritual warfare that was raging in contemporary culture. His "war service" was to fight for what he believed to be true. This is why he traveled to Royal Air Force bases in 1940 and 1941 giving lectures on Christianity to servicemen.

Television as we know it was not yet. The first public television broadcasts were made in England in 1927 and in the United States in 1930. Regular broadcasting service began in the U.S. on April 30, 1939, in connection with the opening of the New York World's Fair. Scheduled broadcasting was interrupted by World

War II, and not until after the war was service resumed by a few broadcasting stations.

World War II brought many things to the United Kingdom, and one was a new openness to religion. The complacency toward organized religion, often found in a time of peace, was shattered, as were the foundations of many lives. Most people were still reading books, and all of a sudden Christian publishers found people ready to read books on religion.

C. S. Lewis did become a scholar and writer. Together his books have sold millions of copies. For example, *The Problem of Pain* published in 1940, had already undergone twenty hard-cover printings by 1974 and continues to be a best-seller. *The Screwtape Letters* was reprinted eight times before the end of 1942, and the paperback editions were at one million by 1987. C. S. Lewis Societies continue around the world, especially in the United States; they hold regular meetings to read and discuss his work. Books about Lewis are also popular, as is almost any information about the man.

What is important about C. S. Lewis is that he was committed to defending and helping us understand basic Christianity. A writer for *Harper's* magazine once said: "The point about reading C. S. Lewis is that he makes you sure, whatever you believe, that religion accepted or rejected means something extremely serious, demanding the entire energy of the mind." By the late 1980s, the annual sales of the fifty or so books Lewis wrote approached two million dollars a year, with about half accounted for by the Narnia chronicles. Millions of people have been affected by reading Lewis's books.

At the end of 1946, there were twelve television stations operating on a commercial basis in the United States; by 1948, there were forty-six stations, and construction had begun on seventy-eight more, with more than three hundred applications submitted to the Federal Communications Commission for permits to build new stations.

# A Biographical Timeline of Clive Staples Lewis

| | |
|---|---|
| 1898 | Clive Staples Lewis born in Belfast, Ireland, on November 29, the second son of Albert James Lewis, a solicitor, and Flora Augusta Hamilton Lewis. Brother, Warren, was three years older. |
| 1905 | The family moved to "Little Lea," a large new house. Lewis later wrote: "I am the product of long corridors, empty sunlit rooms, upstairs indoor silences, attics explored in solitude . . . also of endless books." |
| 1908 | Mother, Flora, died of cancer on August 23. Lewis prayed for God to keep his mother alive. When she died, he blamed God. |
| 1908– 10 | In September 1908, both Lewis brothers were sent to England to Wynyard (Belsen) to school, in Watford, Hertfordshire. This was a terrible experience, in part, because of a brutal headmaster who was later declared insane. |
| 1910 | That autumn Lewis attended Campbell College near his home in Ireland for half a term. He left because of illness and because his father did not like the school. |
| 1911 | From January 1910 to the summer of 1913, Lewis returned to England to attend a preparatory school named Cherbourg House (Chartres) in Malvern. During this period, Lewis decided he was no longer a Christian. He became quite "worldly," discovered Wagner's music, and began to write poems and political history. |
| 1913 | Lewis won a classical scholarship to Malvern College and attended from September 1913 to July 1914. He wrote an atheistic tragedy in Greek form. He came to hate the school and had his father take him out. |
| 1914 | In the spring Lewis met Joseph Arthur Greeves. They became lifelong friends and corresponded through letters for forty-nine years. |
| 1914– 1916 | Lewis studied with W. T. Kirkpatrick, who helped prepare him for entrance to the University of Oxford. He studied Greek, Latin, French, German, and Italian. He also read in English and American literature, listened to music, and wrote poetry and romance in prose. |
| 1915 | In October, he read George MacDonald's *Phantastes*. MacDonald was to have a great impact on his later life. |

# A Biographical Timeline of Clive Staples Lewis

| | |
|---|---|
| 1916 | In December he sat for a classical scholarship at Oxford and was admitted to University College. He loved it. |
| 1917 | From January to March Lewis continued to study under Kirkpartick. His lack of ability in mathematics caused him to fail. On April 28, he went to Oxford; but before the end of term, he was recruited into the army to serve in World War I. During this time he made friends with E. F. C. (Paddy) Moore and later with his mother, Janie King Moore. Later, when Paddy was killed, Lewis became a son to Mrs. Moore, who was a widow. This relationship continued until 1951 when she died. On September 25, 1917, he was commissioned a second lieutenant in the Somerset Light Infantry. He arrived on the front lines of France on his nineteenth birthday. |
| 1918 | He was hospitalized in January, suffering from trench fever. He rejoined his battalion on March 4 and brought in about sixty German soldiers as prisoners. He was wounded in action at Mount Bernenchon and again went to the hospital on April 14. On May 22, he returned to the hospital in England. On June 16, he was released from the hospital and went to visit the Kirkpatricks at Great Bookham. |
| 1919 | In January he returned to University College, Oxford, and began to make many lifelong friends, including Owen Barfield, a student at Wadham College, Oxford. He published *Spirits in Bondage*, his first book, a small collection of lyric poems, under the name of Clive Hamilton. |
| 1920 | In the spring he took a First-Class Honours degree in Mods. from Oxford University. |
| 1921 | Lewis made his first visit to W. B. Yeats' home on March 14. |
| 1922 | In April he began to write *Dymer*, a long narrative poem. He also began a verse version of *Till We Have Faces*. He took an Oxford First-Class Honours degree in Greats. |
| 1923 | He took an Oxford First in English and won the Chancellor's Prize. |
| 1924 | He began tutorial work at University College in philosophy for one year. |

# A Biographical Timeline of Clive Staples Lewis

1925     He was elected to a Fellowship in English Language and Literature at Magdalen College, Oxford, where he stayed until 1954. His friends included J. R. R. Tolkien, Nevill Coghill, H. V. D. Dyson, and A. C. Harwood, who later became members of the Inklings.

1926     Under the pen name Clive Hamilton, he published a book-length narrative poem *Dymer*. He claimed the story "arrived, complete" when he was in his seventeenth year.

1929     During Trinity Term, the third term of the academic year, Lewis confessed on his knees at Magdalen that "God is God." In September Lewis's father died in Belfast.

1930     In October Lewis and Mrs. Moore and her daughter settled at The Kilns, which was to be his home until his death.

1931     Lewis and his brother started out on motorcycle to visit a zoo thirty miles east of Oxford. He later said that when they started out he did not believe that Jesus Christ was the Son of God but when they reached the zoo he did. He was thirty-three years old.

1933     *The Pilgrim's Regress: An Allegorical Apology for Christianity, Reason and Romanticism* was published.

1936     *The Allegory of Love: A Study in Medieval Tradition,* for which he won the Hawthornden Prize, was published. Shortly after, Lewis and Charles Williams began correspondence, which led to a close friendship.

1937     Lewis won the Gollancz Memorial Prize.

1938     *Out of the Silent Planet* was published.

1939     *The Personal Heresy: A Controversy*, a debate with E. M. W. Tillyard, master of Jesus College, Cambridge, was published. Lewis believed poetry should be objective and impersonal. Oxford University Press moved to Oxford, and Charles Williams, who worked for the press, also came to Oxford. Lewis and Williams remained close friends until Williams' death on May 15, 1945.
           *Rehabilitations and Other Essays*, a collection of studies of English writers, of British education, etc., was published.

1940     *The Problem of Pain* was published.

# A Biographical Timeline of Clive Staples Lewis

| | |
|---|---|
| 1940– 1941 | Lewis was the wartime lecturer on Christianity for the Royal Air Force. |
| 1941 | Lewis helped form the Socratic Club at Oxford and became a longtime president. On August 6, Lewis began his first of twenty-five talks on the BBC radio. |
| 1942 | *Broadcast Talks: Reprinted with Some Alterations from Two Series of Broadcast Talks ("Right and Wrong: A Clue to the Meaning of the Universe" and "What Christians Believe") Given in 1941 and 1942*—later revised, these become the first two parts of *Mere Christianity*. *The Screwtape Letters* was published. Also *A Preface to 'Paradise Lost', Being the Ballard Matthews Lectures Delivered at University College, North Wales* was published. |
| 1943 | *Christian Behaviour: A Further Series of Broadcast Talks* was published. Later, in revised form, it became the third part of *Mere Christianity*. *Perelandra* was published. *The Abolition of Man, or Reflections on Education with Special Reference to the Teaching of English in the Upper Forms of Schools* was published, originally three lectures at Durham University. |
| 1944 | *Beyond Personality: The Christian Idea of God* was published. Later revised, it became the last part of *Mere Christianity*. |
| 1945 | *That Hideous Strength: A Modern Fairy-Story for Grown-ups* was published. This was the last volume in the "science fiction" trilogy. |
| 1946 | Lewis was awarded the doctorate of divinity by St. Andrews University. He published *George MacDonald: An Anthology*. MacDonald probably had a greater impact on Lewis than any other writer. |
| 1947 | *Miracles: A preliminary Study* was published. |
| 1948 | *Arthurian Torso: Containing the Posthumous Fragment of "The Figure of Arthur" by Charles Williams and a Commentary on the Arthurian Poems of Charles Williams by C. S. Lewis* was published. |
| 1949 | *Transposition and Other Addresses* was published, containing some of Lewis's finest essays. The American title was *The Weight of Glory and Other Addresses*. |

# A Biographical Timeline of Clive Staples Lewis

| | |
|---|---|
| 1950 | *The Lion, the Witch and the Wardrobe* was published—the first of the seven Chronicles of Narnia children's stories. Lewis was fifty-two years of age. |
| 1951 | *Prince Caspian: The Return to Narnia* was published, the second Chronicle. Lewis was offered the honor of Commander of the Order of the British Empire by the prime minister, but he kindly refused. Mrs. Moore died. |
| 1952 | Doctorate of literature awarded Lewis, *in absentia* by Laval University, Quebec, on September 22. *Mere Christianity* and *The Voyage of the 'Dawn Treader'* were published, the third Chronicle. Reepicheep, the gallant mouse is seeking Aslan's country. |
| 1953 | *The Silver Chair* was published, the fourth Chronicle. |
| 1954 | *The Horse and His Boy* was published, the fifth Chronicle. *English Literature in the Sixteenth Century, Excluding Drama*, originally in the Clark Lecture series at Trinity College, Cambridge, was published. |
| 1954 | Lewis left Oxford after almost thirty years to accept the professorship of medieval and Renaissance literature at Magdalene College, Cambridge. |
| 1955 | *Surprised by Joy: The Shape of My Early Life*, his autobiography detailing his life up to 1931, was published. *The Magician's Nephew* was published, the sixth Chronicle. |
| 1956 | *The Last Battle* was published, the seventh Chronicle of Narnia. In a legal ceremony Lewis and Joy Davidman Gresham were married on April 23. Lewis and Joy later had an "ecclesiastical marriage" in January 1957. Joy had cancer of the thigh. |
| 1958 | *Reflections on the Psalms* was published. |
| 1960 | *The Four Loves* was published. *Studies in Words*, lectures given at Cambridge, were published. An American publisher brought together seven essays as *The World's Last Night and Other Essays*. On July 13, two months after they returned from a visit to Greece, Joy died. |
| 1961 | *A Grief Observed* was published under the pen name of N. W. Clerk. Also published was *An Experiment in Criticism*. |
| 1962 | *They Asked for a Paper: Papers and Addresses* was published. |

# A Biographical Timeline of Clive Staples Lewis

1963    In July Lewis went into a coma but recovered. He resigned his professorship at Cambridge. On November 22, C. S. Lewis died at The Kilns only seven days short of his sixty-fifth birthday.

1964    *Letters to Malcolm: Chiefly on Prayer* was published posthumously. It was the last book Lewis prepared for the press.

## INTRODUCTION TO *MIRACLES*

Lewis talked and wrote a lot about miracles during the early 1940s. In fact, he started his book on miracles in 1943. People had told him that the miracles in the Gospels were hindrances to their belief. For him, Christianity was precisely the story of a great miracle and was nothing without the supernatural. But also during this time many materialists and liberal theologians dismissed miracles as unhistorical and unscientific. Lewis's defense of miracles was important in his day and for ours.

Members of several churches proclaim that C. S. Lewis was a member. In fact, denominationalism was unimportant to C. S. Lewis. While he preferred to attend the local Anglican church, this was more a matter of convenience than of conviction.

*Miracles: A Preliminary Study* was first published in 1947 by Bles. In the book Lewis set up a philosophical framework for the approach that supernatural events—miracles—can happen in our world. Starting with the focus of the possibility of miracles in general, he built a solid and powerful argument for the acceptance of divine intervention. As with so many of C. S. Lewis's books, *Miracles* has become a classic in our time and is still considered one of the finest on the subject, even by some agnostic philosophers. But not everyone agrees with this assessment. George Sayer said that even though *Miracles* is the most philosophical and most carefully considered of Lewis's books, "it is one of the least successful, primarily because its main argument is suspect. The argument is based on a distinction between naturalism and supernaturalism.

In the naturalist system, everything is caused by and dependent on everything else. Such a system, therefore, has no such thing as free will or rational judgment. Lewis argued that, if human reasoning is invalid or, neither valid nor invalid, but determined in a context in which validity has no meaning, then all belief in science and philosophy is also invalid." If this is so, faith in the naturalist system is also invalid, and naturalism is self-contradictory.

Sayer went on to write that Lewis believed "what we call reason makes it possible for us to alter nature. But human reason cannot be explained by rational or naturalistic causes; rather, it must come from a self-existence reason, a supernatural reality that can be called God." The same would apply to moral judgments. They could not be valid as part of a naturalistic system with no free will. Lewis argued that moral judgments "are based on human conscience, which is an incursion into nature of a self-existent moral wisdom."

Also in the mid-1940s in Oxford was a lively and growing debating society called the Socratic Club. C. S. Lewis was the club's president, and it developed into a forum in which arguments for and against religion were presented. Lewis gave at least eleven main speeches before the club as well as consistently taking part in the debate from the floor. These were interesting times in Oxford, and many famous people—and others who would become famous years later—participated in or attended these debates.

The only time Lewis was "bested" in argument was on the occasion of the famous debate on the evening of February 2, 1948, with the Oxford

*Natural law*—In ethics, the idea that there are, within each person, natural moral laws known by all, moral order divinely implanted and accessible to all human beings by way of reason. All beings, potential or actual, come under the regulation of this eternal law. All things are inclined toward their proper acts and ends by divine reason. Both people and animals share in this divine regulation. To avoid confusion with the law of nature, Lewis called natural law "the eternal law," which applied especially to the free acts of people, the "natural moral law." Natural law is not made by human reason but is naturally implanted in the reason of humans by God—Miethe, *The Compact Dictionary of Doctrinal Terms.*

philosopher, G. E. M. Anscombe, a woman and a Roman Catholic. The audience did not agree on who had won the debate, but Lewis felt his argument that naturalism was self-refuting had been proved wrong. After the debate, Lewis modified that particular chapter in *Miracles*. Interestingly, Elizabeth Anscombe did not share Lewis's feelings. Many years later, when told of Lewis's response to the debate, she was surprised and upset. She had no idea he had taken the debate so seriously. She had been playing the role of a contemporary philosopher, not expressing her deepest beliefs.

Many students were able to hear Lewis at his reflective, logical best during these debates, and the memories often lasted a lifetime. While still an undergraduate at St. John's College, Oxford, Antony G. N. Flew, the famous atheist philosopher, attended this debate and recorded his memories of the event and of seeing Lewis and Anscombe leaving with their opposite countenances—him with head hung low, and her, not normally given to such displays, skipping with delight—as they walked down the dark street in Oxford that night.

## MIRACLES

**CHAPTER 1: THE SCOPE OF THIS BOOK**

### *Chapter at a Glance*

Chapter 1 is only three pages. The question of whether miracles occur cannot be answered by experience. Neither can it be answered by history, by examining the evidence by rules of historical inquiry. It's a philosophical question—a question of the worldview a person holds.

Aristotle (384–322 B.C.) was one of the most influential philosophers in Western history. He was Plato's prize pupil, tutor to Alexander the Great, and wrote on every major subject in philosophy: metaphysics, philosophy of science, philosophical psychology, aesthetics, ethics, and politics. He is the father of classical logic.

### *Summary*

Lewis opened the chapter with a quote from Aristotle's *Metaphysics*, Book II, "Those who wish to succeed must ask the right preliminary questions." Then he told a ghost story. He had only met one person who claimed to have seen a ghost. The interesting thing about this was that the person didn't believe in an immortal soul before she saw the ghost and still disbelieved after seeing it. She thought it a trick or illusion of the nerves. Seeing is not always believing.

Lewis's example shows that we can always explain away or reinterpret experience. When and how we do this will depend on our presuppositions. If this is so with direct experience, how much more so with historical inquiry. Neither direct experience nor historical inquiry can prove that there are miracles. They can only provide evidence if a person believes miracles are possible.

We see these kinds of moves in New Testament interpretation. Some New Testament scholars rule out the possibility that the Gospel of John was written in the mid first century. They say a much later date is required because Jesus is represented as predicting Peter's execution. Their presupposition is that predictive prophecy is impossible. So John's Gospel must have been written after Peter's death.

*Miracles* is a philosophical analysis of miracles which would precede any investigation of whether particular miracles *have occurred*.

The work that Lewis has done in *Miracles* has significant consequences for how we study and interpret the Bible. Some interpreters discount or explain away the miracles in the Bible. When

How would you know that a miracle has happened? What would convince you that a miracle has actually happened?

they do so, they may be assuming at the outset that there are no miracles. It's not their inquiry into the biblical text that leads them to the conclusion that this or that miracle did not happen.

Logical positivism was the philosophical mode of the day, and linguistic analysis was gaining popularity. Logical positivism held that all statements about moral or religious values are scientifically unverifiable and, therefore, meaningless.

 **COMMENTARY**

The story Lewis told about the woman and the ghost is reminiscent of A. J. Ayer's near-death experience. Ayer, one of the leaders of logical positivism, wrote "What I Saw When I Was Dead." He related that he had encountered an intensely bright red light that was painful even when he turned away from it. This light for him represented the governance of the universe. His entire experience, he believed, indicated that death was not the end of consciousness. In spite of his experience, he remained an atheist.

## CHAPTER 2: THE NATURALIST AND THE SUPERNATURALIST

### Chapter at a Glance

Lewis says there are two broad views of reality. One view is that nature is all there is. A second view is that there is something in addition to nature. Lewis calls those who hold the first view naturalists and those who hold the second supernaturalists.

What evidence should be allowed to count for or against the existence of God? or for or against Christianity? What would it take, or did it take, for you to believe in God, or to become a Christian? How would one search for such evidence?

### Summary

The naturalist believes the "ultimate Fact" is that the universe is operating on its own, by itself. Further, the naturalist believes that every event is tied to another event, that every event happens because some other event happened, and all are ultimately tied to the "Total Event." All existing things and happenings are totally interlocked and cannot be independent from the whole event. Nothing really exists on its own.

A supernaturalist agrees with the naturalist that something exists in its own right, that there exists some fact necessary to explain all others. This fact is a necessary ground for everything else. But, of course, the supernaturalist doesn't think this "fact" is nature. Everything ultimately falls into two categories: (1) Either things or one thing is basic and originally exists on its own. (2) The second category is full of things that derive from, come from, result because of, the one thing which is basic and causes all other things to exist. Therefore, this one thing is self-existent, exists on its own. Everything else exists only because the one thing exists and would cease to exist if the one thing stopped maintaining the others in existence.

What do you think it means to refer to the "sovereignty of God"? How does this idea relate to the idea of humans having freedom of the will?

Lewis compared the two views by saying that the naturalist gives a democratic picture of reality, while the supernaturalist gives a monarchical—governed by a king—picture. For the supernaturalist, sovereignty does not reside with the whole mass of things but with the one thing. The supernaturalist believes that the one self-existent thing is on a different level and is more important than all other things.

The one self-existent thing is what supernaturalists call God. But there is an important distinction here. The essential difference between naturalism and supernaturalism is not exactly the same as believing in a God and total disbelief. Naturalists could admit to a certain kind of God, a "great cosmic consciousness" or a "God" which arises from the whole process. Lewis didn't think a naturalist would object to this kind of God because it would not be outside of nature or exist on its own.

If there is reason to believe that nature is not the only reality which exists, then we certainly can't say in advance that it is secure from intrusion, from miracles. However, if naturalism is true, we can know absolutely that miracles are not possible. How could something come into nature from outside it when there is *nothing* outside! Yes, some events may be mistaken for miracles because of our ignorance. The first choice that must be made is between the two views, between naturalism and supernaturalism.

 COMMENTARY

Naturalism and supernaturalism are two all-encompassing worldviews. Naturalism believes that physical reality is all there is and that everything can be explained on the basis of how physical particles interact. The supernaturalist believes that physical reality is derivative. It is dependent on a more basic reality which is spiritual and which Lewis identifies with the God of Scripture. In subsequent chapters Lewis will compare these two worldviews and how well each explains our experience best (p. 20).

## CHAPTER 3: THE CARDINAL DIFFICULTY OF NATURALISM

### *Chapter at a Glance*
A totally adequate worldview must be able to explain, in principle, everything there is. And so this is a requirement of naturalism. If there are events or objects that cannot be explained by reference to the totality of physical particles and their interactions, naturalism would be an inadequate worldview.

Lewis's strategy in the present chapter is to point to realities with which we're all familiar, that can't be explained by reference to the totality of physical reality.

Napolean complained to Laplace that he had left God out of his system, to which Laplace replied, "I have no need of that hypothesis."

The naturalism Lewis is arguing against is stated clearly and succinctly by the French physicist and mathematician, Pierre-Simon Laplace (1749-1827). Laplace maintained if we knew (1) the state of the universe at any given moment and (2) the laws of nature, we could predict the entire future of the universe.

What is the reality that naturalism can't explain? Lewis says it is reasoning—one of the foundations on which philosophy and science rest.

When we set forth a theory or an entire worldview, such as naturalism or theism, we offer reasons for what we are claiming to be true. We bring forth evidence in support of the claim and make inferences from that evidence.

Lewis's central claim in this chapter is that naturalism can't account for reason on which naturalism depends.

As we listen to people talk, we often judge their reasons as good and bad. As a simple example, Lewis takes a dog. Ryan makes a claim: (1) Fido is dangerous.

We ask Ryan how he knows that to be true. Ryan says: (2) Fido is muzzled and (3) Visitors go out of their way to avoid Fido.

Richard also claims, (1) Fido is dangerous. We ask Richard why he makes this claim. He says, (4) Fido is black.

Most people listening to Ryan and Richard's reasoning would say that Ryan has good reasons for his belief, while Richard doesn't have good reasons.

Richard believes that all black dogs are dangerous because he was bitten by a black dog when he was a child. We call this kind of belief irrational and in so doing distinguish it from rational, well-founded beliefs.

Naturalists recognize and make use of this distinction between rational and irrational beliefs. Where we believe a person's assertion is based on an irrational belief, we discount it. If a man suffering from delirium tremens claims there are snakes in the house, we put no stock in what he says. Whereas if a man known to be rational makes the claim, we exercise caution as we move through the house.

Both Marxism and Freudianism use this line of reasoning to discount statements of various people. Marxism says a person's beliefs are conditioned by his place in the social structure. Marxists discount some statements by a person from the middle class as irrational.

Lewis says there are no exceptions to this in our everyday dealings. If the belief is based on something irrational, we don't give credence to it.

Lewis argues that Naturalism is committed to the view that every belief is a result of irrational causes. Every belief is ultimately the result on the totality of nature. The totality of nature is irrational. Therefore, every belief has an irrational cause including the well-argued beliefs of the naturalist.

Houston A. Craighead has recast Lewis's argument in a clearer and more straighforward form:

1. Any belief that is held solely on the basis of non-rational causes is a belief that that is not held with rational justification.
2. If Naturalism is true, then all of our beliefs are held solely on the basis of non-rational causes.
3. The Naturalist believes that Naturalism is true.
4. The Naturalist's belief in his own view is not rationally justified.

This is the inherent contradiction in Naturalism. Even if Naturalism is true, believing it is not rationally justified.

 COMMENTARY

Naturalism is a comprehensive worldview that aims to explain all reality. In this chapter, Lewis has pointed to a part of reality than Naturalism can't explain: human reason which Naturalists value highly and appeal to in setting forth their worldview. But if their position is true, we have no reason to believe it. Another kind of worldview is required to provide an account of human reason.

## CHAPTER 4: NATURE AND SUPERNATURE

### *Chapter at a Glance*

Lewis says that if his argument put forth in chapter 3 is sound, nature and reason are two kinds of realities that interact but neither of which is reducible to the other. The great vision of naturalism is that reason could be reduced to nature but Lewis has just argued that that isn't possible.

When Nature invades Reason, it diminishes reason. Examples of this are when emotion takes over, when substances such as alcohol affects the brain or a tumor affects normal functioning of the brain.

On the other hand, Reason acts on Nature and adds value by doing so.

Reason which exists in finite human beings comes and goes. When we sleep, our reason is interrupted.

If Reason doesn't owe its existence to Nature, where does it come from? Lewis argues that it owes its existence to a being that is eternal and self-existent. This being we call God.

At this point, Lewis has argued that there are two basic realities—Reason and Nature. They interact but neither can be reduced to the other. What is their relationship to the whole of reality?

Some have seen both Nature and Reason as existing eternally. This is a view Lewis calls Dualism. And while he says this view seems to hold promise for explaining the existence of evil, he doesn't see that this is a coherent concept.

Another approach taken by some naturalists is to say that the universe produces a cosmic consciousness. When all of the elementary particles of nature are in certain configuration, a cosmic consciousness emerges. This cosmic consciousness may even impart conciousness to finite creatures.

But, according to Lewis, this approach has the same problems that he identified previously. If this cosmic consciousness has irrational causes—that is, a certain configuration of nature as a whole—we will discount its beliefs in the same way we disount the beliefs of a man suffering from delirium tremens.

"Every object you see before you at this moment—the walls, ceiling, and furniture, the book, your own washed hands and cut finger nails, bears witness to the colonisation of Nature by Reason: for none of this matter would be in these states if Nature had had her way"—C. S. Lewis, *Miracles*.

Lewis implies that if we are to guarantee the validity reason and distinguish valid and invalid inference, we must see reason as existing independently of nature.

Could it be that nature and reason both exist eternally? Nature doesn't produce reason and reason doesn't create nature. This is a view called dualism. Lewis says he has difficulty with seeking how two eternally existing realities could interact in the way that reason and nature do in individual human beings.

"In the beginning, God created the heavens and the earth" (Gen. 1:1).

The most plausible way of understanding the relationship between Reason and Nature is to say that Reason is a self-existent being. We call this self-existent being God, who created nature.

 **COMMENTARY**

Lewis tells us much that is very important about the "Unsymmetrical Relation" between reason and nature. One not only has to account for life itself on the basis of matter alone but also for intelligent life. Perhaps they are not the same thing. Certainly intelligent life is more than just life. But can the more complex come from the less complex? Can we believe that simple living things over millions of years simply developed intelligence? Is man merely the most sophisticated of machines, or is he essentially different from any conceivable feedback mechanism? Does man's knowledge of the brain support the claim that human reasoning corresponds to mechanical processes?

Reason itself is evidence for the supernatural. Many aspects of the mind, or intelligence, are hard to account for on the basis of a pure mechanism or naturalism: (1) Our minds can work with the material world without being controlled by it; we have free will. (2) Morals must be integrated with a material world as well. We act as if some things are right and some are wrong. (3) Human beings have values that are not manmade. (4) Human beings have an aesthetic experience that separates us from the animal world. (5) Human beings have religious experience that confirms meaning and purpose in the universe. God makes Himself known both in the natural order and in human experience.

To explain these away as a result of a mechanistic evolutionary process is to reduce these experiences to much less than they are in reality.

## CHAPTER 5: A FURTHER DIFFICULTY IN NATURALISM

### *Chapter at a Glance*
Moral judgments present a further difficulty for naturalism. The fundamental moral principles on which all others hang are rationally received. Nobody pays attention to any moral judgment that can be shown to spring from nonmoral and nonrational causes. If naturalism is true, then the idea of "I ought" has no objective meaning. Many naturalists are delighted to admit that there is no such thing as right or wrong. But they behave as though there is right and wrong.

### *Summary*
Logical thinking or reasoning is the "pivot" of the argument against naturalism because it is the only assertion the naturalist can't deny without philosophically cutting his own throat. Again, you cannot prove that there are no proofs. Yes, all human ideals can be thought of as illusions and all love as "biological by-products," but a real question exists as to whether

" . . . that which is known about God is evident within them: for God made it evident to them" (Rom. 1:19, NASB).

you can do so without "extreme un-plausibility," without holding a picture of things no one really believes.

But men don't just reason about factual matters; they also make judgments about moral matters (for example, about whether this or that "ought" to be done, or if it is "good" or "evil"). There have been two views regarding moral judgments. (1) Some think that another power other than reasoning is being used when moral judgments are made. (2) Others think that moral judgments are also made by reason. Lewis accepted the second view, that the fundamental moral principles on which all others hang are rationally received. Remember, axioms cannot be proved, but that doesn't make them irrational. Rather they are "self-evident" and the basis of all other proofs.

These axioms of moral reasoning are such that "their intrinsic reasonableness shines by its own light. It is because all morality is based on such self-evident principles that we say to a man, when we would recall him to right conduct, 'Be reasonable'"—C. S. Lewis, *Miracles*.

For the purpose of this discussion, which view one adopts with regard to moral judgments is not relevant. What is important, however, is to realize that, as with other thoughts, moral judgments cause the same sort of difficulty for naturalism. The very fact that two men can differ about good and evil and that moral differences are hotly debated shows precisely that principle is being used. In "real life" no one seriously regards any moral judgment shown to originate from nonmoral and nonrational causes.

Think about the word *ought*. How do you explain its force?

If the reality that such ideas as "ought" and "ought not" can be thoroughly explained by irrational and nonmoral causes, then those ideas are merely illusion. Naturalists explain how such illusions originated by positing the process of chemical conditions producing life, natural selection producing consciousness, thus conscious organisms behaving in one way live longer, have offspring, and pass on behavior. This builds up a "pattern of behavior" which eventually results in tribal conformity, the invention of gods who punish moral departures, and, through time, a powerful impulse to conform develops. Yet there is one small problem. Because one impulse is often at odds with others, mental or moral conflict arises. "I want to do this, but I ought to do that."

This story may or may not explain why moral judgments are made, but it doesn't explain how one could be right in making such judgments. Lewis went so far as to say: "It excludes, indeed, the very possibility of their being right." If naturalism is true, the very concept "I ought" has no objective meaning. For that matter, no "moral judgments" would have meaning except about one's own personal feelings which would be mistakenly taken as statements about the real moral quality of actions. And certainly the naturalist can, according to his position, consistently agree that there is no such thing as right or wrong. Lewis reminded us that many naturalists are "delighted" to admit this.

Once this is admitted, that all ideas of good and evil are hallucinations, they must stick with it, but most naturalists do not do so. In the next instant they are admonishing people to work for posterity, education, this or that revolution, or to live and die for the good of humanity. We are reminded that a naturalist like H. G. Wells spent his long life arguing for such things with "passionate eloquence and zeal." Very odd indeed!

Lewis thought that the naturalists sometimes forget. While they continue to hold a philosophy which excludes humanity, they yet remain—or try to remain—human. The "sight

"For [Naturalist's] write with indignation like men proclaiming what is good in itself and denouncing what is evil in itself, and not at all like men recording that they personally like mild beer but some people prefer bitter. Yet if the 'oughts' of Mr. Wells and, say, Franco are both equally the impulses which Nature has conditioned each to have and both tell us nothing about any objective right or wrong, whence is all the fervour? Do they remember while they are writing thus that when they tell us we 'ought to make a better world' the words 'ought' and 'better' must, on their own showing, refer to an irrationally conditioned impulse which cannot be true or false any more than a vomit or a yawn?"—C. S. Lewis, *Miracles*.

of injustice" makes them throw their naturalism to the winds and speak like men of genius. They seem to be saying in one breath, as it were, that morality *is* an illusion, but we are urging you to adopt conditions of behavior which will preserve the human race.

But one cannot escape via this route. The only way we can consistently continue to make moral judgments is to believe that human conscience is not nature's product. Morality makes sense only along an entirely different line, that it is the result of an absolute moral wisdom, existing absolutely "on its own." The last two chapters have led us to acknowledge a supernatural source for both (1) rational thought, and (2) for our ideas of good and evil. We now know more about God. We are just about ready to begin the main argument of the book. But first, some "Answers to Misgivings."

 COMMENTARY

Yes, moral judgments cause a great problem for naturalism. As Lewis argued all his life, there must be a universal moral law, or all disagreements and moral criticisms would be meaningless. Absolute morality can only reside in a mind, which is the source of whatever is true in our moral judgments—a mind whose thoughts are the standard of truth and falsehood alike in morality and in respect to all other existence. In short, objective morality more than implies belief in God.

## CHAPTER 6: ANSWERS TO MISGIVINGS

### Chapter at a Glance

Certain misgivings must be addressed. No one disagrees that rational thinking is conditioned by the brain. Yes, moral ideals are connected to history, environment, and economic structure. However, the rational and moral element of each mind is a "point of force" which originates with the supernatural and works its way into nature. Rational and moral elements are conditioned by the mechanism of the brain or nature but not originated by it.

Another misgiving is the idea that if the supernatural exists it would need no argument at all to support it, it would be so obvious. But Lewis will show that the supernatural is so easily overlooked because it is so obvious. For example, naturalists are busy thinking about nature, not about the fact that they are thinking. In reality the supernatural is not remote and obscure but ever present.

### Summary

Lewis strongly agreed that rational thinking can be shown to be conditioned in its exercise by the brain, a "natural object," that such thinking can be impaired by alcohol or a thump on the head. Rational thinking ceases when the brain stops functioning.

The rational and moral element is conditioned by the mechanism of the brain or nature but not originated by it. Rational thought always involves a state of the brain, but reason is more than "cerebral bio-chemistry."

Lewis turned to another possible misgiving: the argument of some that if the supernatural exists, then it should not need argument at all. It should be as obvious as the "sun in the sky." Lewis has "great sympathy" for this view. However, two things must be noticed.

"Our question is not: can we believe in our freedom on the basis of what we know of physiology, but quite the other way round: Do these facts of our experience create an embarrassment for theoretical physiolgy?"
—Donald M. MacKay in *Brain and Conscious Experience,* Spring Verlag, 1966.

1. Imagine looking at a garden through a window upstairs. Yes, it is obvious that you are looking through a window, but if it is really the garden you are intent on, which really interests you, it could be a long time before you think of the window. Or, reading this book, obviously with your eyes, but you can read for hours without once thinking about the eyes.

Naturalists are busy thinking about nature, not about the fact that they are *thinking*. Lewis argued that when we pay attention it is obvious that our thinking cannot be simply a natural event, that something other than nature exists. In reality "the Supernatural is not remote and abstruse." Rather it is an experience which is always with us, "as intimate as breathing."

2. "The state of affairs in which ordinary people can discover the Supernatural only by abstruse [complex] reasoning is recent and, by historical standards, abnormal." Because of a "century or so of Naturalism" ordinary men are forced to shoulder burdens which they were never expected to bear before. Ordinary men must find the truth themselves or go without.

There may be two explanations for this change: (1) Perhaps, humanity, in rebelling against custom and authority has made a "ghastly mistake." (2) Or, perhaps, the power which governs humankind is carrying out a "daring experiment." If a daring experiment, it may be intended that the whole mass of the people should now occupy those heights once reserved only for the sages. Perhaps the very distinction between "wise and simple" is to disappear because all are not expected to become wise. If this is true, our present condition could appropriately be called "growing pains." But we must be clear about "our necessities." For if an individual doesn't "obey wisdom in others," or venture forward toward it himself, this is fatal.

The chapter closes by addressing one more possible misgiving. But, first, we are reminded that reasons have been given for believing that a "supernatural element" exists in every rational person. Thus, the fact of human rationality in our world is a miracle by the definition in chapter 2. But this is not all that is meant by *miracle*. The reader is asked to be patient. Thus far, human reason and morality have been used as proofs of the supernatural. But we may find that the "very nature of nature" is to endure "*this invasion*," that the very nature of nature is to bear miracles in general.

Later on the book is concerned with what everyone calls "miracles." "Does Supernature ever produce particular results in space and time *except* through the instrumentality of human brains acting on human nerves and muscles?" The term *particular results* is used because nature as a whole is one massive result of the supernatural. Nature was created by God, and God maintains nature's existence. But does He ever do anything else to nature? Does He ever introduce into nature events that are not simply the working out of the general character He gave to nature in the beginning? Such events would be what are popularly called miracles. This meaning of *miracle* will be used in the remainder of the book.

"In fact, though by this time you ought to be teachers, you need someone to teach you the elementary truths of God's word all over again. You need milk, not solid food! Anyone who lives on milk, being still an infant, is not acquainted with the teaching about righteousness. But solid food is for the mature, who by constant use have trained themselves to distinguish good from evil. Therefore let us leave the elementary teachings about Christ and go on to maturity, not laying again the foundation" (Heb. 5:12–6:1).

# COMMENTARY

When Lewis mentioned the recent change in the state of affairs by which ordinary people can discover the supernatural, he said that perhaps the masses of people are now to occupy the heights once reserved only for the sages, that maybe all are expected to become wise. What an incredible insight into the nature of Christianity and, ultimately, into the doctrine of priesthood of all believers! How can you be what you are not? How can you teach what you do not know? Paul said in Hebrews 5:12–6:1 that we are to leave behind the milk and move on to the meat and the responsibility that comes from this. The question is: Are you ready to partake in the "daring experiment"?

### CHAPTER 7: A CHAPTER OF RED HERRINGS

#### *Chapter at a Glance*

The case against miracles rests on two postulates: (1) God's character precludes miracles, or (2) Nature's character does. The more popular—it is against Nature's character—is discussed first. Two superficial misunderstandings or red herrings are discussed.

The idea of a "red herring" comes from the practice of drawing a red herring across a trail to confuse hunting dogs. It is something that distracts attention from the real issue. Make a list of things that distract us from the important issues in Christianity today. Do you see other examples in *Miracles*?

#### *Summary*

The chapter starts by telling us that from having admitted the existence of God as Creator of nature, it doesn't follow that miracles must or can happen. It might be against God's character to perform miracles. Or nature may have been created so that it cannot be modified. Thus, the case against miracles rests on these two different premises: (1) Either God's character excludes them, or (2) nature's character does. Lewis treated the second premise first because it is "more popular." Two forms of the idea that nature's character precludes miracles, which are "very superficial" and could be labeled as "misunderstandings or Red Herrings," are discussed.

First red herring: It is often said that we don't believe this or that because of the laws of nature. In "olden times" people believed all kinds of things before the laws of nature were known.

The idea that the "progress of science" has changed the question as to whether miracles are possible is closely tied to another idea, that people "in olden times" believed in miracles because they didn't know the laws of nature. They were so naive or simply stupid that they didn't perceive a miracle as contrary to nature. Thus, so goes the argument, early Christians could believe in a virgin birth, but moderns know this is scientifically impossible.

In fact, it turns out that the story of the virgin birth is a particularly striking example of why this theory is nonsense. Look at the biblical story: Did Joseph naively just accept Mary's pregnancy? Not according to Matthew: "Because Joseph her husband was a righteous man and did not want to expose her to public disgrace, he had in mind to divorce her quietly" (1:19). Joseph knew as well as "any modern gynecologist" that in ordinary nature women don't have babies without sexual relations. "In any sense in which it is true to say now, 'The thing is scientifically impossible,' [Joseph] would have said the same." In fact, "When St. Joseph . . . accepted the view that [Mary's] pregnancy was due . . . to a miracle, he accepted the miracle as something contrary to the known order of nature."

The very word *miracle* implies excitement, fear, and wonder. Miracles are taken as evidence of supernatural power and precisely that the laws of nature have been suspended in that case. Miracles couldn't have been seen as surprising

"An angel of the Lord appeared to him in a dream and said, 'Joseph son of David, do not be afraid to take Mary home as your wife, because what is conceived in her is from the Holy Spirit. She will give birth to a son, and you are to give him the name Jesus, because he will save his people from their sins'" (Matt. 1:20–21).

unless they were viewed as exceptions to the rules. And, if you don't know the rules, you won't see something as an exception. We must know what is ordinary before anything will seem extraordinary. Belief in miracles is only possible in so far as those laws of nature are known. Obviously, if one starts by ruling out the supernatural, no miracles will be permitted or perceived.

Second red herring: Many maintain ancient people could believe in miracles because of their false concept of the universe—with the earth at the center and man the most important being. It seemed reasonable, so the argument goes, in "olden times" to then suppose a Creator who was interested in man and would interrupt nature for our advantage. (This may even be more reasonable today!) But now that we know the unimaginable vastness of the universe (as a mental construct), it becomes ridiculous to believe that people on this tiny (hardly more than a) speck could be so important.

Ptolemy—Claudius Ptolemæus, was a second century A.D. mathematician, astronomer, and geographer, born in Egypt. He lived in Alexandria in A.D. 139, and was probably still alive in 161. He invented a planetary theory, the discovery of the distress of the moon's orbital motion due to the attraction of the sun, and has the singular distinction of being the sole astronomer of antiquity whose works survive. The mathematical theorems of the Greek Hipparchus (190–120 B.C.) and Ptolemy remain the basis of trigonometry today.

This view is factually inaccurate, whatever its value as an argument. More than seventeen hundred years ago Ptolemy knew that with regard to the stars the Earth was a point with no magnitude. The insignificance of the Earth was "commonplace" to people in history. Lewis gave the examples of Boethius, King Alfred, Dante, and Chaucer. Statements in modern books to the contrary are due to historical ignorance—or, we might add, intellectual dishonesty.

The real question is why the "spatial insignificance" of our earth should in modern times suddenly become a "stock" argument against Christianity when for some fifteen centuries this fact has been asserted by Christian philosophers, Christian poets, and Christian moralists without the least suspicion of any conflict with Christian theology. First the strength of the stock argument is considered. The truth is that it doesn't matter whether the universe is vast and filled with other bodies or empty, except for our own. Either position could be *used* as an argument against Christianity. God is treated such that whatever He does is used in evidence against Him. But, in fact, this kind of objection to Christianity isn't really based on the observed nature of the actual universe at all.

The argument is, in fact, meaningless. Man *is* a finite creature, one who has sense enough to know he is finite. Because of this fact, on any view one can hold meaningfully, man finds himself dwarfed by the whole of reality.

"When I consider your heavens, the work of your fingers, the moon and the stars, which you have set in place, what is man that you are mindful of him?" (Ps. 8:3–4).

Really there is no question of whether all that is exists for man (supposed "religious" view) or not (supposed "scientific" view). Lewis said either way, God or nature, of course it does not exist for us. So both the arguments, the supposed "religious" view and the supposed "scientific" view end in the same place: self-existent nature or God. Christianity doesn't imply that all things were made for man, but it certainly does involve believing that God loves man, became man for our sake, died, and rose from the dead for us.

# COMMENTARY

The origin and destiny of the universe and the question of whether miracles have occurred is not the proper jurisdiction of science as science. Individual scientists bring to their work

"A God who is trustworthy is the guarantee to the scientist that natural events will not break precedents unless God has a special reason to do so; the scientist can thus rely from day to day on his expectation, based on the systematic observation of precedent which we call science"— Donald M MacKay, *Science and the Quest for Meaning*, (William B. Eerdmans Publishing Company, 1982), 48.

philosophical and theological presuppositions that shape the way they do science.

Scientific method assumes that there are patterns in nature that can be discovered. There is no contradiction in assuming that God created these patterns and gave human beings the capacity of discovering them. God who created these patterns has the capacity to introduce other patterns into His creation.

## CHAPTER 8: MIRACLES AND THE LAWS OF NATURE

### *Chapter at a Glance*

Are supernatural interferences with nature possible or impossible? Both naturalists and supernaturalists agree that nature is generally regular. The only question is, If you grant the existence of God outside nature, are miracles intrinsically absurd? Three conceptions of the laws of nature are discussed. It is inexact to define a miracle as some act that breaks the laws of nature. A miracle is not an event without cause or result. The legitimate "demand" that all reality be "consistent and systematic" doesn't rule out miracles.

### *Summary*

This chapter is to address the question: Is Nature such that supernatural interferences are impossible? Both sides agree that nature is generally regular. Conceding the existence of God outside nature, the real question is whether there is any "intrinsic absurdity" in the belief that He can intervene to produce within nature events which the regular "going on" of the whole natural system would never have produced.

There have been three conceptions of the laws of nature: (1) These laws are regularities we observe but we don't know why they are as they are and we can't see why the opposite should not be the case. (2) The laws of nature are applications of the law of averages. Nature's groundwork is random and lawless. However, the sheer number of "units" is so immense that they can be discerned with "practical accuracy." What are called "impossible events" are so overwhelmingly improbable—"by actuarial standards"—that they needn't be taken into account. (3) The fundamental laws of physics are really "necessary truths" as in mathematics. That is, if we understood precisely what we're saying, we would see that the opposite would be meaningless nonsense. The fundamental laws of nature are just statements that every event is itself.

It is, or should be, clear that the first concept of the laws of nature gives no guarantee against miracles. If there is no notion why a thing happens, then we can't have any notion of why it happens, or no reason why it shouldn't be otherwise. Also we can have no certainty that it might not be different tomorrow or the day after. The second theory, based on the law of averages, is in the same spot. This is akin to a coin being tossed over and over again. The longer you toss, the more nearly equal the number of heads and tails. But those who believe in miracles are "maintaining precisely" that the coin "is loaded." The second view will work only if nature hasn't been interfered with (as it were). So it actually "begs the question."

With regard to miracles, at first glance, the third view of the laws of nature as necessary truths seems to "present an insurmountable obstacle." For to break them would be self-contradictory and not even God can do what is self-contradictory. But is this really so? Are the laws of nature really necessary truths?

Begging the question—A fallacy in logic/reasoning, which is committed when a person uses as a premise for his argument the conclusion he intends to prove. Example: "Shakespeare is a greater writer than Parker Hayden because people with good taste in literature prefer Shakespeare. How can I tell who has good taste? Anyone who prefers Shakespeare." The conclusion states only what has already been asserted and does not establish the truth of its conclusion.

A rather long discussion follows, with several examples, of what happens to the laws of nature when "interferences" come into the picture. For example, if a billiard ball happens to hit a "roughness in the cloth." The law is still true: billiard balls will behave in a particular way. But, though interferences leave the law perfectly true, the interference changes the outcome.

We have here an important insight: No miracle can break the laws of nature if they are necessary truths, but then no miracle needs to break them. The laws of nature in advance cannot take into account, or rule out beforehand, the introduction of a new factor into the situation, namely supernatural force.

"If God annihilates or creates or deflects a unit of matter He has created a new situation at that point. Immediately all Nature domiciles this new situation, makes it at home in her realm, adapts all other events to it. It finds itself conforming to all the laws"—C. S. Lewis, *Miracles*.

What the laws of nature really are should now be a little clearer. We talk as if they cause events to happen, but this is not so. They don't start the billiard balls moving. They only analyze the motion after something else has provided it.

It is inexact to define a miracle as some act which breaks the laws of nature. The moment an event which comes from beyond nature enters nature's domain it obeys all its laws. Examples include miraculous conception causes pregnancy, inspired books become subject to textual corruption; even miraculous bread is eaten and absorbed. Miraculous events do not suspend the pattern of nature indefinitely but immediately upon entering nature feeds new events into the natural pattern. Nature is an expert hostess.

"God is not in need of anything, but all things are in need of Him"—Marcianus Aristides (530–468? B.C.)

## COMMENTARY

Miracles are not some act that breaks the laws of nature. They are events that come from beyond nature. But once they come into nature, they obey all natural laws. Lewis gave several important examples to show that miraculous events don't suspend the pattern of nature indefinitely but immediately upon entering nature feed into the natural pattern. The real problem for many is not miracles as such but the fact that if they exist, then they have to examine what exists outside of nature and may have to be responsible to that power of force, to God.

## CHAPTER 9: A CHAPTER NOT STRICTLY NECESSARY

"For since the creation of the world God's invisible qualities—his eternal power and divine nature—have been clearly seen, being understood from what has been made, so that men are without excuse" (Rom. 1:20).

### *Chapter at a Glance*

Chapter 9 deals with a purely emotional objection to miracles. If supernature is responsible for creating nature, then nature doesn't exist on its own and loses all spontaneity. Before Lewis became a Christian, he couldn't bear the idea that nature had been put there to amuse him or, worse, to point to a moral lesson. The exact opposite is true with regard to the reality of nature: To say that God created nature is not to say nature is unreal but exactly that nature is real. Nature is partly good and partly evil because nature has been corrupted. Nature, like humankind, is to be redeemed.

"For we know that the whole creation groans and suffers the pains of childbirth together until now" (Rom. 8:22, NASB).

### *Summary*

This chapter treats a purely emotional objection to miracles which weighed heavily on Lewis at one point. Lewis thought that the idea that nature had been made and could be altered by God took away all the spontaneity he found so refreshing. To him the idea that nature had been made was suffocating. He even wrote a poem—most of which he had forgotten—about a sunrise, indicating his desire that the world existed by chance with no Spirit behind it.

Every person has weaknesses, but ironically often a person's strength proves to be the greatest weakness. As contradictory as this may sound, when you are at your weakest you must be strongest! In such times, which try the depths of one's soul, you must especially turn to God for His strength and power. Use your weaknesses; aspire to your strengths!

Lewis "could not bear" the sense that the sunrise had been "arranged" or "had anything to do with oneself." He certainly didn't want to think it had all been put there either to amuse him or, worse, to point to a moral lesson. If nature proves artificial, where will you go to seek wildness? Is there a real out-of-doors? The "cure of this mood" had begun, for Lewis, years before writing *Miracles*. However, it was not complete until he started studying the question of miracles.

 **COMMENTARY**

When we see nature for what nature really is, we offer neither worship nor contempt. We must also remember that nature, like ourselves, is to be redeemed. Nature has been subjected to a "vanity" which was a disease, not an essence. Nature will, again like us, be "cured in character" but not tamed or sterilized. The old enemy/friend will be "so perfected as to be not less, but more, herself, but not the same. And that will be a merry meeting."

**CHAPTER 10: "HORRID RED THINGS"**

*Chapter at a Glance*
Some believe that all forms of supernaturalism present a childish and unworthy notion of God and so they reject all such views, especially Christianity.

Lewis tried to distinguish between the core or real meaning of Christian doctrines and caricatures of those doctrines derived from the language in which they are stated. But the miraculous is not one of the things which drops away from the real meaning. It is the core itself scraped as clean of inessentials as possible.

### Summary

The study of nature provides no security against miracles precisely because nature is only part of reality, perhaps but a small part. From invasion from outside, nature has no defenses. But many, wrote Lewis, who don't believe in miracles, admit all this. Their objection to miracles comes from another direction. They believe that the supernatural would not invade. And those who believe the supernatural has invaded have a "childish and unworthy notion" of God. Thus, all forms of supernaturalism that assert such invasions, and especially Christianity, are rejected by these objectors.

A surface look at Christianity seems to imply a view of reality which has been steadily refuted by the expansion of knowledge in the last two thousand years such that no honest person could return to today, objects the critic of miracles.

This impression accounts for the contempt or even disgust many have for Christians. Being convinced that Christianity implies a "local 'Heaven,' a flat earth, and a God who can have children," the atheist is impatient with Christianity's solutions and defenses. Further, these critics wonder if Christian theology would have ever come into existence if the New Testament writers had had the slightest knowledge of what the real universe is actually like. This was how Lewis himself used to think before he became a Christian. He remembered "from within" the attitude of the skeptic.

Lewis gave two examples of mental pictures to distinguish thinking from imagining: (1) of the whole of London with several million people as compared to his image when he thinks of London by way of a mental picture of Euston Station; and (2) when we say the sun is ninety-odd million miles from earth. We can't really have a mental picture of the totality of the real London or the distance to the sun. Our "clear *thinking* is accompanied by *imagining* which is ludicrously false to what we know that the reality must be." To "think" is different from to "imagine."

Now we need to add to the previous statement that thinking may be sound in certain respects where it is accompanied not only by false images but also by false images mistaken for true ones. Lewis discussed the child who thought all poisons contained "Horrid Red Things" inside. A third situation must also be examined. The first two examples were concerned not with language but with thought and imagination.

Often when talking about something not discernible via the five senses, words are used which, in one meaning, refer to things or actions that are experienced through the senses. For examples, we *grasp* an argument, *see* the point, or *follow* what is being said. But in none of these cases do we *actually* grasp, see, or follow. We all know this "linguistic phenomenon" referred to as "metaphor." Metaphor is not optional, a way poets or speakers decorate their work or speech which isn't needed.

Next Lewis offered three guiding principles: (1) Thought is different from the imagination which accompanies it. (2) Thought may be sound even when the false images that accompany it are

"All that concerns the un-incarnate activities of God—His operation on that plane of being where sense cannot enter—must be taken along with imagery which we know to be, in the literal sense, untrue. But there can be no defence for applying the same treatment to the miracles of the Incarnate God. They are recorded as events on this earth which affected human senses. They are the sort of thing we can describe literally"— From *God in the Dock* (William B. Eerdmans Publishing Company, 1970) , 71.

mistaken for true ones. (3) Anyone who converses about things which can't be seen must ultimately talk as *"if they could be"* seen.

All this has to be applied to the "savage" or "primitive" beliefs of the Christian faith. Before going on, however, Lewis admitted that many Christians, but certainly not all, do have in mind the crude mental pictures which horrify the unbeliever. But it has now been shown that the simple presence of such mental pictures doesn't say anything with regard to the reasonableness or folly of the thoughts that go with them. Everyone would be thinking nonsense all the time if absurd images meant absurd thought. Mature Christians no more believe that the Father has a human form than that the Son literally came down from heaven.

Now a "rather simpleminded illusion" is handled. Some suggest Christians get rid of the mental pictures and the language which suggests them. Lewis maintained that this is impossible. When we try to get rid of anthropomorphic images, we only succeed in exchanging images of another kind. He recounted the statement: "I don't believe in a personal God, . . . but I do believe in a great spiritual force." But *force* brings in images about winds, tides, electricity, and gravitation. We are mistaken to think we are safe from this "degree of absurdity."

For contemporary adult Christians, then, the absurdity of the images doesn't imply absurdity in doctrine.

Lewis addressed the difference between "explaining" and "explaining away," which is indicated in two ways: (1) Some conclude, when referring to a thing as being meant "metaphorical" that it is hardly meant at all. Examples include carrying the cross, hell "fire," and the Fall in Genesis. Christ spoke metaphorically when He told us to carry the cross. This is true, but from this they wrongly conclude that "carrying the cross" means only leading a respectable life and giving to some extent to charities. Lewis pointed out that metaphorical Christian doctrines mean something just as "supernatural or shocking" after the ancient imagery is removed. (2) Such metaphorical statements involve both the supernatural, unconditioned reality and events on the historical level, which interference with nature is held to have produced. The first (the supernatural, unconditioned reality) is in fact "indescribable in 'literal' speech and must be interpreted metaphorically. The second, events on the historical level, can be talked about literally. If they happened in history, they were perceived by man's senses. When we start applying metaphorical interpretations to such events, explanation degenerates into "explaining away."

The chapter ends by reminding us that nothing in it helps us make a decision about the probability or improbability of the Christian claim. All that has been done in chapter 10 is to remove a misunderstanding so a fair hearing to that question may be secured.

# COMMENTARY

It is unquestionably true that what separates Christianity from other religions is that it *is* precisely the story of a great miracle. It is impossible to separate any aspect of Christianity, such as its moral teaching, or Christianity as a whole from the miraculous elements contained in it. One is reminded of Thomas Jefferson, who was at once both a genius and a person who couldn't see the implications of his own thoughts (for example, "all men are created equal, . . . endowed by their Creator with . . . unalienable Rights, . . . Life, Liberty, and the pursuit of Happiness," and yet he owned slaves until the day he died). However, the deist Thomas Jefferson made an even "greater" mistake. In 1819, he began isolating the passages from the Bible which he believed to be the authentic words and teachings of Jesus. This resulted in what is now called *The Jefferson Bible*. Of course, much of what he took out were the miracle stories. But this is precisely the core of Christianity!

## CHAPTER 11: CHRISTIANITY AND "RELIGION"

### *Chapter at a Glance*

Many people seem interested in talking about beauty, truth, and goodness or a God who is simply an indwelling principle of them. But the God of today's popular religion would do no miracles. In chapter 11, Lewis evaluated the evidence for pantheism.

### *Summary*

The type of "god" of today's popular religion would almost surely do no miracles. But the question is whether such a popular religion is likely to be real. Many folks have a "friendly interest" in speaking about "beauty, truth and goodness" or a god who is simply the indwelling principle of them. But mention a God who has purposes, performs particular actions—a concrete, choosing, commanding, prohibiting God with a real character—and they become embarrassed or angry. They think this conception of God is primitive and crude, even irreverent. The popular religion of our day is pantheism, and Lewis examined its credentials.

*Deism*—From the Greek theos, "God," which is transliterated into Latin as "Deus." The earliest known use of the term *deism* was in 1564. Generally, it is belief in a God who created the world out of nothing but now is uninvolved with the world or its events. He governs through unchangeable, eternal laws, and is in no way imminent in creation. Deists were strong in America in the 1700s and taught the superiority of human reason over faith, revelation, and miracles. They opposed any established church and believed in religious freedom and the separation of church and state, as did many Christians. Several of the founding fathers were deists: Thomas Jefferson (1743–1826), Thomas Paine (1737–1809), Ethan Allen (1738–89), Benjamin Franklin (1706–90), and George Washington (1732–99).

Pantheism—From the Greek pan, "all," and theos, "god," the worldview that denies God's transcendence. It teaches that the substance of God and the substance of the physical universe are in some sense identical; reality is composed of a single being of which all things are modes, moments, members, appearances, or projections. Classical Hinduism is pantheistic, as were the philosophies of Benedict Spinoza (1632–77) and G. W. F. Hegel (1770–1831) —Miethe, *The Compact Dictionary*.

Pantheism is generally based on a "fanciful picture" of religion in history. Man concocts "spirits" to explain natural phenomena. In the beginning these invented spirits are much like man himself, but as man progresses, they become less anthropomorphic and in the end what is left is a pure abstraction—mind or spirituality. God is no longer a particular entity with real character and becomes simply "the whole show."

Of course, this "imagined history" of belief is not authentic. Pantheism, it turns out, is compatible to us, not because it is the last stage in a slow evolution of enlightenment, but because it is old indeed, perhaps the most primitive of religions.

Far from being the "final religious refinement," pantheism is the perpetual natural inclination of the human mind. Only Platonism, Judaism, and Christianity are capable of resisting pantheism. Lewis believed that pantheism was nearly as strong in his day as it was in ancient India or Rome. "Theosophy" and worship of the life-force are both forms of pantheism.

The pantheist says that we are all dependent on and are intimately related to God. The Christian agrees. But for the pantheist this means that we are "parts" of Him or are contained in God. By "dependent on" and "intimately related" to God, the Christian means He is our Maker and we are His creations. The pantheist believes that God is equally present in both evil and good and is indifferent to both. The Christian, on the other hand, believes this is far too simple. God is present in a great many different modes, but He is not present in matter as in man. He is present in some men more than others. And He is in Jesus like no other man.

In each detail Christianity corrects the natural anticipations of pantheism and offers something more difficult—so much so that eventually the pantheist changes his argument and no longer accuses Christians of childish naiveté, but now accuses us of "pedantic complexity" and "cold Christs and tangled Trinities." And this "continuously troublesome" nature of Christianity, when faced with popular "religion," is as it should be. Lewis gave examples: a real musician is troublesome to a man who wishes to indulge in untaught music appreciation, as is the real historian to one who only wants to romanticize about "the old days."

If God created the world, then He must be the source of all concrete, individual things and events. And, if this is so, then God Himself must be concrete and individual in the greatest proportion. Nothing else could be concrete and individual unless the origin of all other things were itself so. There is no conceivable means that what is abstract or general could produce concrete reality. If *anything* is to exist, the original thing must be an utterly concrete fact, not a principle or a generality, much less an ideal or a value.

To say that God is a "particular Thing" needs to be put into context, too. The balance needs to be brought back. "Derivative things"—atoms to archangels—hardly exist at all when compared with their Creator. Their principle of existence is not in themselves. If we fully understand *what* God is, we see that there is no question *whether* He is. It is impossible that he not exist. But once He has created, we must say that He is a particular thing. This does not diminish Him; on the contrary it helps us to see in Him a positive perfection obscured in pantheism, the perfection of being creative. God is "brim-full" of existence. God can give existence away, cause things to be, and be different than Himself.

Like created beings, God has specific characteristics. God invents, acts, and creates. It would be silly to assume in advance that He doesn't do miracles. Now we have to ask: Why do the mystics talk about Him as they do? "And why are many people prepared in advance to maintain that, whatever else God may be, He is not the concrete, living, willing and acting God of Christian theology?"

The reason is that "great prophets and saints" have an intuition of God that is positive and concrete in the highest degree, but in reporting their vision to disciples they have to use many negatives. Then, we lesser mortals understand only the negatives. When we lesser mortals come "limping after" and try to build an "enlightened" religion, we take over these negatives (concepts like infinite, immaterial, impassable, immutable) and use them uncontrolled by a positive intuition. At each step along the way, we have to strip off of our idea of God some human attribute. But in so doing we reach an incorrect conclusion as if we removed everything we can know about God.

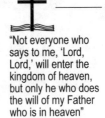

"Not everyone who says to me, 'Lord, Lord,' will enter the kingdom of heaven, but only he who does the will of my Father who is in heaven" (Matt. 7:21).

This is exactly why the scriptural statement that only he who does the will of the Father will ever know the true doctrine is philosophically accurate. Lewis believed that though imagination may help some, it is in the moral life, or through the devotional life, that we touch something concrete. This will immediately begin to correct the growing emptiness of our idea of God.

Yes, we need to reject old images to attempt to do justice to God's moral attributes. But here again we must be careful of analogies. We have trouble thinking of a love which is not passionate, but God has no passions. The analogy of water is used. "Getting wet" happens to our bodies. But God is exempt from passion in the same way that water is exempt from getting wet. God can't be affected with love because He is love.

## COMMENTARY

The pantheist's God doesn't demand, in fact, doesn't do anything. The pantheist's God is like a book on a shelf. You can reach for Him, but He will not pursue you. An impersonal God, a subjective God of beauty, truth, and goodness, existing only inside our heads is well and good. You have all the "convenience" of a "god" without any of the "mess."

But a living, personal God approaches us as hunter, king, and husband. It is one thing to look for God as a child might play at burglars, but it is quite another matter to hear an unexpected *real* footstep or to find the real God. Lewis said it is sort of a "Rubicon"—once it is crossed there is no going back. You may cross or not, but once one does there is no security against miracles.

### CHAPTER 12: THE PROPRIETY OF MIRACLES

#### *Chapter at a Glance*

Would the living God work miracles? Many of sincere piety feel He would not because doing such would be unworthy of Him. This idea is founded on an error. Miracles are not exceptions or irrelevancies but precisely the thing the entire story is about.

"My teaching isn't Mine, but is from the One who sent Me. If anyone wants to do His will, he will understand whether the teaching is from God or if I am speaking on my own" (John 7: 16–17, HCSB).

Rubicon—The river forming part of the boundary between Gaul and Italy whose crossing by Julius Caesar in 49 B.C. was regarded by the Senate as an act of war. To "cross the Rubicon" is to make an irrevocable commitment.

"As the heavens are higher than the earth, so are my ways higher than your ways and my thoughts than your thoughts" (Isa. 55:9).

### Summary

If the "Ultimate Fact" is the living God, not an abstract or opaque idea or thing, then He may do things, might work miracles. But would He? Lewis said that many people of "sincere piety" feel that God would not do miracles. Doing such would be "unworthy of Him." He would be like a "petty and capricious tyrant" who breaks his own laws. Only an "incompetent workman" produces work needing interference. The assurances given in chapter 8 will not help such people. They feel it impious to suppose that God should sometimes unsay, or undo, what He has once said, or done, with such magnificence. This belief comes from "deep and noble" mental sources and must be treated with respect. Nevertheless, Lewis said this idea is founded on an error.

At some length Lewis related how a schoolboy who has just learned the rules may over use them and really cannot be expected to see why they are not absolute and can be broken to advantage. Rules exist behind the rules. There is a unity deeper than uniformity. And we are in no position to judge God's use of them. To be sure, the gap between His mind and ours is incalculably greater than that between Shakespeare's mind and his critics.

We must be careful when we try to interpret God's external act or acts as seen from within nature. The normalities of nature are real. But to think that an agitation of them would constitute a flaw of the living rule and natural unity by which God works (and from His view) is a mistake. If miracles occur, we may be sure that *not* to have them would be the real inconsistency. Indeed, the miracle would be the highest consistency. Dorothy Sayers made this point clear in her "indispensable book," *The Mind of the Maker*. Much of the modern objection to miracles is founded on the suspicion that they are marvels of the wrong kind. Even the Resurrection can be viewed as a desperate, final attempt to save the Hero from a spot which is out of the Author's control. But miracles are not like that.

 **COMMENTARY**

If miracles have occurred, it is precisely because they are what the entire story is about. Miracles are not exceptions (though they may be rare) or irrelevancies. They are exactly, in detail, those chapters on which the plot turns in this great story. God has written a long story, containing a complicated plot, and we must be seriously vigilant readers—though often we are not.

## CHAPTER 13: ON PROBABILITY

### *Chapter at a Glance*
Chapter 13 tells us that even though we should accept only miracle claims for which historical evidence is sufficiently good we still need a criterion for deciding the intrinsic probability of the claim. The modern historian is likely to accept the most improbable natural explanations rather than say a miracle occurred. Is this right or fair? We must sort out the different kinds of improbability.

### *Summary*
The argument in *Miracles* thus far has shown two things: (1) that they are possible, and (2) that there is nothing "antecedently ridiculous" in accounts that God has sometimes done miracles. Of course, this does not mean all miracle stories have to be believed. Lewis asserted that

lies, exaggerations, misunderstandings, and hearsay possibly make up more than half of all of what has been said and written. A criterion to judge any individual miracle story must be found. The criterion is plain in a way: accept miracle stories for which the historical evidence is "sufficiently good." But, as seen from the beginning in *Miracles,* the answer to this question is going to depend on "How far is this story intrinsically probable?"

We are told the common course of "the modern historian, even if he allows the possibility of miracle, is to admit no particular instance of it until every possibility of 'natural' explanation has been tried and failed." This sounds all well and good, but then Lewis goes on: "That is, he will accept the most improbable 'natural' explanations rather than say that a miracle occurred."

David Hume (1711–66) was a Scottish empiricist and skeptic who was born and died in Edinburgh. He wrote on philosophy, religion, the history of England, letters, and economics. Hume is a minor figure in the history of philosophy, but some think he was one of the most important philosophers who ever lived. His thought is often used today to argue against the possibility of miracles and the existence of God.

Is this right or fair? Can we start by knowing in advance that the most improbably natural event is more probable than any miracle? The different kinds of improbability must be sorted out. By definition miracles are rare and therefore improbable, but this does not make a story that a miracle *has* happened inconceivable. That kind of improbability is true of all events—pebbles dropped from the stratosphere over London hitting any one spot, a certain person winning a large lottery. We are not here concerned with "antecedent probability of chances," only with historical probability.

Since David Hume's famous discussion "Of Miracles" in his *An Enquiry Concerning Human Understanding*, historical statements about miracles are believed the most improbable of all historical statements. Hume thought probability rested on what can be called the "majority vote of past experiences." Further, the regularity of nature is supported by something even better, the unanimous vote of past experiences, by "firm and unalterable experience." Thus, for Hume there was "uniform experience" against miracles. The probability that witnesses were lying or mistaken is always stronger than that a miracle actually occurred.

If there is absolutely uniform experience against miracles, then we must agree with Hume; that is, if miracles have never happened, why then, they never have. But Hume was arguing in a circle. We can know that experience against miracles is uniform only if we know that all reports of miracles are false. But we can know all reported miracles are false only if we know already that miracles have never occurred.

A deeper problem with, or objection to, Hume is the whole idea of probability as Hume understood it. For Hume, probability depended on the principle of the uniformity of nature, the assumption that nature always proceeds in the same way. But we cannot know the uniformity of nature by experience. Christian and non-Christian agree that nature is generally regular. Yet all the observations people have made or will make cover only a small fraction of the events that actually happen. The truth of the matter is that we assume the uniformity of nature. We cannot prove it either by the past or by the future. The odd thing about all this is that Hume knew this as well as anyone. His *Essay on Miracles* is entirely inconsistent with the more radical skepticism of the rest of his work.

Do miracles occur? And is the course of nature absolutely uniform? are the same question asked in two ways. Hume treated them as different. Hume said, yes, nature is absolutely uniform, and no, miracles do not occur. Hume never actually discussed the real question at all.

At best, if we stick to Hume's method, we get a total draw on the question. Hume's kind of probability holds only within the frame of uniformity, when that is itself the question. Thus, ultimately, Hume is no help. We must, then, look for some different kind of probability. We need to ask why people believe in the uniformity of nature. Three reasons are given, two of which are considered irrational: (1) We are creatures of habit. New situations are expected to look like old ones. We share this with animals and often see it working with "comic results" in them. (2) We are a "planning" species, and when plans are made, we have to leave out of consideration the possibility that tomorrow nature may not act as it did today. Even if we thought for a moment about the possibility, there would be nothing we could do about it, so why bother? The picture of uniformity dominates our minds, and we assume it. Both beliefs are irrational and could be used to build up a false or true belief. (3) Lewis quoted Sir Arthur Eddington: "In science we sometimes have convictions which we cherish but cannot justify; we are influenced by some innate sense of the fitness of things." This, suggested Lewis, is no doubt the source for our belief in the uniformity of nature. "A universe in which unprecedented and unpredictable events were at every moment flung into Nature would not merely be inconvenient to us: it would be profoundly repugnant."

Is this faith or preference in uniformity a thing that can be trusted, or is this just the way our minds work? Does this sense of fitness correspond to anything in external reality? It all

"Loving the Lord our God with all our mind must include using our minds in a search for the patterns according to which events in his universe are reliably predictable. The more we know of these, the better foresight we can exercise as responsible stewards"
—Donald M. MacKay, *Science, Chance, and Providence,* (Oxford University Press, 1978), 10.

depends on the metaphysics one holds. If nature is all that exists and "our own deepest convictions" are only the by-products of an illogical process, then there isn't the smallest foundation for assuming that our sense of fitness and faith in uniformity tell us anything about a reality outside us. Wonder of wonders, if naturalism is indeed true, there is no reason to trust our conviction that nature is uniform.

This sense of fitness can be trusted only if the deepest thing in reality is in some degree like us. If it is a rational spirit from which we derive our rational spirituality, then our conviction can be trusted. Following Alfred North Whitehead, whom Lewis referred to as "our greatest natural philosopher," the sciences, themselves, require this kind of metaphysic. Whitehead pointed out that centuries of belief in a God who combined "the personal energy of Jehovah" with "the rationality of a Greek philosopher" first produced the solid expectation of systematic order which made possible the birth of modern science. Men became scientific because they expected law in nature, and they expected law in nature because they believed in a legislator. But in most modern science this belief is dead. It will be interesting to see how long assurance in uniformity survives the death.

If God is admitted, must miracles be also? The answer is clear: There is no "security" against it. In fact, this is the only way to have any real belief that nature is uniform normally. If you try to make nature absolute, you can't even assure that uniformity is probable. If we claim too much with regard to nature, we actually get nothing. Theology "offers . . . a working arrangement, which leaves the scientist free to continue

Alfred North Whitehead (1861–1947), British born mathematician and philosopher, taught mathematics in London from 1914 to 1924, when he went to Harvard to teach philosophy until he retired in 1938. Among his most important philosophical works are the *Principia Mathematica*, 3 vols. (1910–13) with Bertrand Russell; *An Enquiry Concerning the Principles of Natural Knowledge* (1919); *The Concept of Nature* (1920); *Science and the Modern World* (1926); *Religion in the Making* (1926); *Symbolism* 1928; *Process and Reality* (1929); and *Adventures of Ideas* (1933). The principle of relativity in physics is the key to understanding metaphysics.

51

his experiments and the Christian to continue his prayers."

Here we find what we have been seeking, a criteria by which to judge the "intrinsic probability" of a supposed miracle. Miracle claims must be judged by this "innate sense of the fitness of things." This is the same sense of fitness that caused us to anticipate an orderly universe. However, we know that miracles are possible on philosophical grounds. Of course, this sense of fitness doesn't replace the need for close examination of the historical evidence. But, the historical evidence, as Lewis has repeatedly pointed out, can only be estimated, if first the intrinsic probability of the recorded event has been estimated.

In giving weight to the sense of fitness of things, we are doing nothing new. This is the principle always used. The three chapters that follow present the central miracles of the Christian faith to show their "fitness." If successful, the fitness of the miracles will become apparent in studying them.

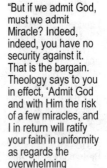

"But if we admit God, must we admit Miracle? Indeed, indeed, you have no security against it. That is the bargain. Theology says to you in effect, 'Admit God and with Him the risk of a few miracles, and I in return will ratify your faith in uniformity as regards the overwhelming majority of events'"
—C. S. Lewis, *Miracles*.

 **COMMENTARY**

Lewis acknowledges that miracles are highly improbable but their improbability doesn't imply that they are impossible. He considers David Hume's well-known claim that miracles are the most improbable of all events. Hume bases this claim on the belief that nature is uniform. But what is the basis of this belief? It can be observation because observation can't establish the uniformity of nature. The uniformity of nature has to be assumed. Since uniformity of nature excludes miracles, Hume is, in effect, assuming that miracles don't happen rather than making a case for this assertion.

## CHAPTER 14: THE GRAND MIRACLE

### *Chapter at a Glance*

Chapter 14 discusses the grand miracle. All other miracles either prepare, exhibit, or result from the Incarnation. If the Incarnation occurred, it is the central event in history. So it must be judged by a different standard. It is easier to argue for the Incarnation on historical than on philosophical grounds. The question is, Does the Incarnation make sense of the "whole work" and remove difficulties that arise elsewhere?

*Incarnation*—From the Latin *in*, "in," and *caro*, "flesh." In theology, this is the doctrine that God, the eternal Son, the second person of the Trinity, became man, or flesh, in the person of Jesus. This does not mean, however, that He gave up His deity in the process (see John 1:14; Rom. 1:3, 8:3; Gal. 4:4; Phil. 2:7–8; 1 Tim. 3:16; Heb. 1; 1 John 4:2; 2 John 7).

### *Summary*

This credibility of the claim that God became man must be judged by a different standard, and Lewis admitted that finding such a standard is difficult. If it occurred, then it is the "central event" in the Earth's history. By Hume's standards, it is infinitely improbable since it happened only one time. The same is true of the whole history of the Earth, but is it incredible? "Hence the difficulty, which weighs upon Christian and atheist alike, of estimating the probability of the Incarnation. It is like asking whether the existence of Nature herself is intrinsically probable." Thus, Lewis wrote that it is easier to argue for the probability of the Incarnation on historical grounds than on philosophical grounds.

The question is, Does the Incarnation make sense of the "whole work" or not? The analogies of a missing part of a novel or a symphony upon which the whole thing really turns are used. Does the Incarnation, though it may have difficulties in itself, continually remove difficulties

"The Word became flesh and lived for a while among us. We have seen his glory, the glory of the one and only Son, who came from the Father, full of grace and truth" (John 1:14).

elsewhere? In the Incarnation we have a "whole mass" of knowledge, and its credibility depends on the extent the doctrine can illuminate and integrate the entire mass of knowledge.

The first difficulty of the doctrine to any critic rests in the very center of it, what is meant when it is pronounced that God became man. How could eternal self-existent Spirit unite with a natural, human, living thing to make one person? This would be a "fatal stumbling-block" except that we have already discovered that every person is more than natural activity, by virtue of his reasoning. However, God's becoming man is not merely another instance of this process. Yet, if we did not know this, have this experience of reason, we could not conceive or imagine the Incarnation.

While we cannot visualize how the divine Spirit abides within the created human spirit of Jesus, we can understand, if the Christian doctrine is true, that our own combined existence is not the sheer irregularity it might seem to be but a dim likeness of the divine Incarnation itself. If God can be part of a human spirit, as in us, and we are a part of nature, then we can get a glimpse of a "new key principle." This is the power of the Higher to come down and include the less.

God "descends to re-ascend" in the Christian story to bring the "whole ruined world" up with Him. We recognize in this descent and reascent a familiar pattern, the pattern of all vegetable life and animal generations. This pattern is also in our moral and emotional life."

If we accept the doctrine of the Incarnation, it puts this principle decidedly at the center. This can be seen in nature because it was put there by God and was first in God. This is not simply a reference to the Crucifixion and Resurrection of God but part of a total pattern of real death and rebirth. Christianity is now compared with the "corn-religions" which were "popular and respectable." There is an odd similarity here. Lewis discussed this whole matter at length.

He concluded that one hypothesis makes everything easy and coherent. The Christian's claim is not simply that "God" was incarnate in Jesus but that the one true God is He whom the Jews worshiped as Yahweh and that it is He who came down to earth. Yahweh has a "double character." First, He is nature's God, her glad Creator. But, second, Yahweh is clearly *not* a nature-God. He is the God of nature.

Elements of nature religion are strikingly absent from the teaching of Christ and from Old Testament Judaism. They present a truth behind nature religion and even behind nature itself. This mention of the Hebrew nation turned Lewis's attention to a feature of the Christian story that is repulsive to the modern mind, the idea of a "chosen people." After knowledge of God has been "universally lost or obscured," God picks one man, Abraham, to be the father of a nation who will carry the knowledge of the true God. Lewis mentioned that the process narrowed even further to one Jewish girl, Mary.

Here we come "perilously near," according to Lewis, to Butler's argument in his *Analogy*. But Lewis was not saying that nature is good. Nor did he say that a god whose actions were no better than nature's would be a proper object of worship for any honest man. The point is much more acute than that. Nature's quality, as far as it affects human life, is neither good nor evil. It permits, on one hand, ruthless competition,

Joseph Butler (1692–1752) entered Oxford in 1715 and studied law and theology. Becoming bishop of Bristol (1738) and of Durham in 1750, he had a lifelong interest in philosophical questions. His *Analogy of Religion* appeared in 1736 and did more to discredit deism than any other book. Butler's argument was empirical and stressed fact in support of religion. The order we find in nature is paralleled by that found in revelation. God is their joint author.

arrogance, and envy; but on the other, modesty and admiration.

The real point is that when we really examine the selectiveness Christians attribute to God we find in it none of the favoritism of which we are afraid. The chosen people weren't chosen for their own sake or for their own honor or pleasure but for the sake of the unchosen. Abraham was told that "in his seed," the chosen nation of Israel, "all nations will be blest."

We now come to a belief deep rooted in Christianity. Lewis called it the "principle of vicariousness." The sinless Jesus suffered for the sinful, and in a sense all good men suffer for all bad men. The vicariousness is also a characteristic of nature. Lewis gave several examples—the cat and mouse, the birds and flowers, parasite and host, unborn child and mother.

It is now seen, as we look back, that the Incarnation has already been brought into contact with four other principles: (1) the composite nature of man which is a fact about the frontier between nature and supernature; (2) the pattern of descent and reascension; (3) selectiveness; and (4) vicariousness. The last three are characteristics of nature. Nearly all religions either reaffirm the facts of nature, give them as they stand a transcendent prestige, negate them, or promise release from such facts and from nature. Several examples are given: the nature religions, life-force worship, and the antinatural or pessimistic religions such as Buddhism or higher Hinduism. Lewis further compared and contrasted nature religions with Christianity.

Christianity sees nature as infected with evil. In nature's operations the great key principles, which exist as conditions of goodness in God,

Vicarious atonement—The Christian doctrine that Christ died in our place to pay the penalty for our sins. The Atonement is that aspect of the work of Christ, particularly His death, that makes possible the restoration of fellowship between God and man which was necessitated because people sinned and became separated from God (see Rom. 3:9–23). Christ bore the punishment justly due all sinners.

take on in nature what Lewis feels driven to summarize as "morbid and depraved." This depravity cannot be totally removed without drastically remaking nature. In the Christian doctrine of redemption not only man, but clearly nature—the planet and beyond—is to be remade or redeemed. We are told the whole creation is in travail, and that man's rebirth will signal nature's. Several problems arise here and the discussion of these attempts to put the whole doctrine of the Incarnation in a "clearer light."

"We know that the whole creation has been groaning as in the pains of childbirth right up to the present time. Not only so, but we ourselves, who have the firstfruits of the Spirit, groan inwardly as we wait eagerly for our adoption as sons, the redemption of our bodies" (Rom. 8:22–23).

The first question is, How does a nature created by a good God get into this predicament, to become imperfect or "positively depraved"? Lewis said the answer to the issue of imperfection is that God created nature in a way as to render it perfection by a process in time. Thus, a degree of evolutionism or developmentalism is inherent in Christianity. But what about nature's depravity? This is all the result of the sins of men and created supernatural beings. Our widespread naturalism makes this doctrine unpopular. For both men and angels, sin was possible because they were created with free will. God surrendered a bit of His authority "because He saw that from a world of free creatures, even though they fell, He could work out (and this is the re-ascent) a deeper happiness and a fuller splendor than any world of automata would admit."

Another question is, If man's redemption is the beginning of nature's, must we conclude that man is after all the most important thing in nature. Lewis was not embarrassed to answer yes. If man is the "only rational animal in the universe," neither his small size nor his small planet would make it absurd to consider him as the "hero of the cosmic drama: Jack after all is the smallest character in *Jack the Giant-Killer*."

Thus far, Lewis has written on the view that the Incarnation was caused only by the Fall. Another view sometimes held by Christians is that the Incarnation would have happened for glorification and perfection even if redemption had not necessitated it. If this second view is taken, then the descent of God into nature would have been the beginning of nature's rebirth. The principle of universal redemption that starts with the redemption of man and moves to nature is more philosophical than any theory which holds that God, having entered nature, should leave it in essence unchanged.

The Christian doctrine of Incarnation entails a certain view of death. The mind naturally adopts two attitudes towards death: (1) the "lofty" stoic view that death "doesn't matter" and should be observed with unconcern, and (2) the natural point of view that Lewis thinks is implicit in almost all conversations, that death is the "greatest of all evils." The Christian view of death is much more subtle. On one side, death *is* Satan's victory, the punishment of the Fall, the last enemy. Jesus detested death, "this penal obscenity," even more than we do. On the other side, to save one's life one must loose it. We are baptized into the *death* of Christ, and it is the cure for the Fall. It is both Satan's and God's "great weapon." It is at one and the same time man's "supreme disgrace" and only hope. Death is, at one in the same time, the thing Christ came to conquer and the means by which it is conquered.

Lewis said that the Christian doctrine of Incarnation entails a certain view of death. What is this view and why is it important? How should a Christian view physical "death," as a victory or as a loss?

The "startling" Christian doctrine of human death is that it is the result of man's sin. Man was originally created without death and once redeemed will again be "immune from it." But, of course, this is "simply nonsense" if man is but a natural creature. If this is what man is, then as we have seen, all thoughts would also be nonsense. Man is a "composite being," a natural organism in a state of *symbiosis* with a supernatural spirit. Currently, the relation of the two parts in the state of symbiosis is "abnormal" or "pathological." In our present state sooner or later the natural element wins and death follows. But according to the Christian view, this was not always the case.

Our present situation, the "frontier-situation," is the odd, unnatural one. Only custom can make it seem natural. But only the Christian doctrine can make it fully understandable. There is a state of war between our natural and spiritual parts.

Accept the Christian doctrine that teaches that man was originally a unity, that the present state/division is unnatural, and all the aspects fall unto place. Yes, human death is the result of sin and the triumph of Satan, but it is also the means of redemption from sin. Lewis called it "God's medicine for Man" and God's "weapon" against the Evil One. It is fairly easy to see how this happened. Satan, the enemy, convinced man to rebel against God. Man lost the power to control his two natures. Thus, Satan produced human death. But God, all the wiser, converted this "penal death" into the means of true eternal life, and thus death must be accepted.

"For since death came through a man, the resurrection of the dead comes also through a man. For as in Adam all die, so in Christ all will be made alive" (1 Cor. 15:21–22).

"Almost the whole of Christian theology could perhaps be deduced from the two facts (a) That men make coarse jokes, and (b) That they feel the dead to be uncanny. The coarse joke proclaims that we have here an animal which finds its own animality either objectionable or funny. Unless there had been a quarrel between the spirit and the organism I do not see how this could be: it is the very mark of the two not being 'at home' together. . . . Our feeling about the dead is equally odd . . . . In reality we hate the division which makes possible the conception of either corpse or ghost"— C. S. Lewis, *Miracles*.

# $\mathcal{SN}$ COMMENTARY

The Incarnation *is* a central, if not *the* central doctrine of the Christian faith. But it is inseparably tied to other essential or fundamental doctrines. How could there be an Incarnation without a preexistent Christ? In the context of the New Testament, how could there have been an Incarnation without the virgin birth? Would any of these make sense without the sinless life of Jesus, and could these have been really testified to without Jesus' death on the Cross and the Resurrection? And, for that matter, how can we know any of the above without a reliable inspired Scripture which tells us about the Second Coming. These are the fundamentals of Christian faith. They are not "in house" niceties which can be accepted or rejected by different individuals or groups who call themselves Christian. They are the core of Christian belief.

## CHAPTER 15: MIRACLES OF THE OLD CREATION

### *Chapter at a Glance*
Christian miracles show that nature hasn't been invaded by an alien power but rather by the God of nature. This puts Christian miracles in a different class. The more we understand God and His purpose, the more plausible miracles become.

### *Summary*
The chapter starts by quoting John 5:19: "The Son can do nothing of himself, but what he seeth the Father do." Christian miracles show that nature has not been invaded by an alien power. They are what might be expected to

happen if nature were invaded by the God of nature, a power which is sovereign. Christian miracles proclaim that God is *the* King of both nature and humankind. This puts Christian miracles in a different class from most others.

Lewis didn't think it was the job of the Christian apologist to disprove all miracle stores which are outside the Christian record. He was not committed to the idea that God has never worked miracles for or through pagans or that God has never permitted angels, "created supernatural beings," to perform miracles. But Lewis claimed that Christian miracles have a much greater intrinsic probability by their organic connection with one another and with the whole structure of the religion they evidence.

"But in your hearts set apart Christ as Lord. Always be prepared to give an answer to everyone who asks you to give the reason for the hope that you have" (1 Pet. 3:15).

In Christianity, the more we understand the God who is present and the purpose for His presence, the more plausible miracles become. Jesus' miracles are classified in two ways, or under two systems with classes. The first system contains six classes of miracles: (1) fertility, (2) healing, (3) destruction, (4) dominion over the inorganic, (5) reversal, and (6) perfecting or glorification. The second system *cuts across the first* and contains two classes: (1) miracles of the old creation, and (2) miracles of the new creation.

Miracles of the old creation duplicate operations we have already seen on the large scale. Miracles of the new creation focus on those that are still to come. Each class carries God's mark. We know this mark through conscience and from nature. Their authenticity is attested by the *style*. Further, it doesn't matter whether Jesus was able to do the miracles He was able to do because He was God or also because He was perfect man. It doesn't matter because it appears that the powers of redeemed man will be almost unlimited.

The real makeup of miracles can be expressed by saying that they are not isolated from other actions in either of the two ways we are inclined to presume. They are not isolated from other divine acts, nor are they isolated "exactly as we suppose" from other human actions. In the first sense, they are close and small and they focus on what God does so large at other times that men don't attend it. In the second, they anticipate powers all men will have when redeemed and when they enter into that "glorious liberty." Thus, Christ is a pioneer not a prodigy. He is the first, though not the last, of His kind.

Lewis returned to his classification and first to miracles of fertility. The first example given is the water turned into wine at the wedding feast in Cana. Lewis said this miracle consists of a shortcut but leads to an event that is the usual one and has a short discussion in support of this thesis. Other examples of miracles in this class are the two involving miraculous feeding, the multiplication of a little bread and fish into much of both. There is a difference here from when Satan tempted Jesus to turn stones to bread. It is different to make more bread out of less. Miracles of fertility are miracles where Jesus duplicates in a supernatural way what God has always been doing in a natural way.

Lewis next addresses the Virgin Birth, a miracle that has been a stumbling block to many moderns. In reality, Lewis contended, the virgin birth is no more or less surprising than any other miracle. Again, we have here a supernatural version of a natural event or process created by the supernatural in the first place. Of course, there was a unique reason for this miracle. However, Lewis thought it out of place here to explore the religious significance of the virgin birth. The point here is simply the miracle and that we have one more witness that here is "Nature's Lord."

Miracles of healing are now in a peculiar position. Humans seem ready to admit that many such healings happen, but they are likely to deny they were miraculous. Lewis says our assessment of whether a healing is miraculous or not will in some part depend on our understanding of the laws of nature at the time. Wise physicians from ancient times until now realize the human body has within it recuperative powers. Their strategy is to remove whatever stands in the way of the patient's healing. When Jesus came, the One who place the recuperative power in the human body was among us.

Sign seen in a physician's examination room: "I treated him but God healed him."

Jesus' only miracle of destruction was the cursing of the fig tree, and it has troubled some. Lewis, however, thought its meaning is "plain enough." The miracle was an "acted parable," a symbol of God's sentence on all that is fruitless and on "official Judaism" of that day. Again, it is an example of "small and close," of what God was doing continually throughout nature.

All the miracles that have been considered so far in this chapter are miracles of the old creation. We see in them all the "Divine Man" focusing for us what God has already done on a larger scale. Miracles of dominion over the inorganic, however, include some that are of the old creation and some of the new. One example of the old creation is when Jesus stills the storm. Lewis said that it is "un-philosophical" to accept the grand miracle and to reject the calming of the storm.

With Jesus' walking on the water, we have an example of a miracle of the new creation. This miracle is a "foretaste" of a nature still in the future. It is an example of the new creation just "breaking in." An interesting observation is made with regard to this miracle: "For a moment it looks as if it were going to spread. For a moment two men are living in that new world. St. Peter also walks on the water—a pace or two: then his trust fails him and he sinks. He is back in Old Nature. That momentary glimpse was a snowdrop of a miracle. The snowdrops show that we have turned the corner of the year." Summer is coming but is still a "long way off." We must remember that winter will not last.

## COMMENTARY

Lewis pointed out that the powers of redeemed man will be almost unlimited. The new man will not be less physical but more physical. Indeed, he will have the spirituality and physicality he was intended to have from the beginning. And his physical and spiritual sides will be in such a proper, wonderful relation that the spiritual will have complete "control," though *control* is perhaps not the best word, over the physical. The new man will have amazing powers, powers we can only guess at now.

For decades theological liberals have seemed to have an inexplicable need almost to make fun of the virgin birth and to consider one of the fundamentals of the faith an "unnecessary miracle." They sometimes try to make something out of the claim that the Gospel of Mark doesn't have a "tradition" of Jesus' virgin birth or conception. Yet Jesus is called the "Son of God" at "strategic places" in Mark's Gospel. Even liberal Stephen L. Harris (*The New Testament: A Student's Introduction*) admitted: "The first reference to Jesus' divine parentage occurs in the opening verse and is addressed directly to readers, who must be aware of Jesus' supernatural identity." If this is not the virgin birth, one has to wonder what it could be. Mark 1:1 reads: "The beginning of the gospel about Jesus Christ, the Son of God." Mark 1:11 tells of the pronouncement of God: "You are my Son, whom I love; with you I am well pleased." And in Mark 1:24 we have the declaration: "Have you come to destroy us? I know who you are—the Holy One of God!" (see also Mark 3:11, 22–28; 5:1–13; 9:8). Certainly statements like these are strongly consistent with the idea of a virgin birth.

"I can understand the man who denies miracles altogether: but what is one to make of people who will believe other miracles and 'draw the line' at the Virgin Birth?...In reality the Miracle is no less, and no more, surprising than any others"— C. S. Lewis, *Miracles.*

How many times does the New Testament have to teach the virgin birth to make it the Christian position? Matthew explicitly affirms that Jesus was virginally conceived (Matt. 1:18–25), and Luke makes it clear (Luke 1:26–38).

## CHAPTER 16: MIRACLES OF THE NEW CREATION

### Chapter at a Glance
Of the miracles of the new creation, only the Resurrection and the Ascension are considered here. We can know little about the new nature, but in some troublesome ways the new nature is interlocked at some points with the old.

Every great religion except Christianity would say that heaven is a state of mind, or spirit. In teaching the resurrection of the body, Christianity teaches that heaven is not just a state of the spirit.

## Summary

The only miracles of the new creation that can be considered are treated in this chapter: the Resurrection and the Ascension. The chapter starts with a review of the qualification for being an apostle. An apostle was someone who had been an eyewitness of the Resurrection, someone who had known Jesus personally before and after His death and could give firsthand evidence of the Resurrection. Acts 1:22 and 2:32, and 1 Corinthians 1:9 are quoted. The first fact in Christian history was the Resurrection of Jesus of Nazareth.

It is important to be clear about what these people who experienced the Resurrection meant. They were claiming that they had all met Jesus during the weeks following His death (either as individuals, as the Twelve, or about five hundred people). The Apostle Paul wrote in 1 Corinthians 15:6, written about A.D. 55, that the majority of the five hundred were still alive when he wrote. All these people were bearing witness to the Resurrection, and this was affirmed by irregular meetings during a limited period. Lewis remarked that the "termination of the period" is important because it is not possible to isolate the doctrine of the Resurrection from the Ascension.

The Resurrection wasn't considered merely or mainly as evidence for the soul's immortality. There was far more to it than that. In rising from the dead, Jesus achieved an event that is the first of its kind in the history of the universe. Jesus' Resurrection was the "first fruits." Jesus "forced open a door that has been locked since the death of the first man. He has met, fought, and beaten the King of Death. . . . This is the beginning of the New Creation: a new chapter in cosmic history has opened."

This doesn't mean the New Testament writers didn't believe in survival. "On the contrary they believed in it so readily that Jesus on more than one occasion had to assure them that He was not a ghost." The fact is, said Lewis, that the doctrines of "the immortality of the Soul," as a Greek or modern Englishman understands it, are entirely irrelevant to the Resurrection because the New Testament writers looked on Jesus' Resurrection as an absolute novelty. What they experienced had nothing to do with the ideas of the soul's immortality, the doctrine of Sheol, or of heaven. Jesus' Resurrection tended to confirm Isaiah 26:19 that the righteous dead "would come back to earth . . . as solid men who cast shadows in the sunlight and made a noise when they tramped the floors."

There are similarities between the risen Jesus and ghosts in popular thought (He appears and disappears at will; locked doors do not stop Him). But, Jesus Himself strongly affirmed that He was physical, eating fish in Luke 24:36–43. Here the modern reader becomes uneasy, and even more so with Jesus' words in John 20:17: "Do not hold on to me, for I have not yet returned to the Father." The uneasiness arises because the story conflicts with what we expect and are "determined beforehand" to read into the account.

What is expected, proclaimed Lewis, is a risen life purely "spiritual" in the negative sense of that word. The word *spiritual* is used to mean not what it is but what it is not—a life without space, without environment, with no sensuous elements. We also tend to "slur over" Jesus' risen

"While they were still talking about this, Jesus himself stood among them and said to them, 'Peace be with you.' They were startled and frightened, thinking they saw a ghost. He said to them, 'Why are you troubled, and why do doubts rise in your minds? Look at my hands and my feet. It is I myself! Touch me and see; a ghost does not have flesh and bones, as you see I have.' When he had said this, he showed them his hands and feet. And while they still did not believe it because of joy and amazement, he asked them, 'Do you have anything here to eat?' They gave him a piece of broiled fish, and he took it and ate it in their presence" (Luke 24:36–43).

*manhood*. We tend to view the Resurrection as a reversal of the Incarnation. All allusions to the risen *body* make us wary.

This new mode of existing, this new body, is like and unlike the body Jesus had before his Crucifixion. It is related to time and space but in a different way. He can eat, be touched, has a history (can be recognized), but He is going somewhere else. This is why the Ascension cannot be disconnected from the Resurrection. The accounts submit that the Resurrection appearances of the risen Christ stopped. They end abruptly in a way that presents greater difficulties to the modern mind than any other part of Scripture. Here we get implications of all those "primitive crudities" to which Christians are not committed.

We cannot just drop the Ascension story because, unlike a ghost, hallucination, or phantom who can just fade away; an actual individual "must go somewhere--something must have happened to it. And if the Risen Body were not objective, then all of us (Christian or not) must invent some explanation for the disappearance of the corpse."

Thus, the Gospels present Christ as passing from death, and after six weeks of appearances, to a mode of existence which has its own nature, a new nature. Jesus said that He was going to prepare a place for us (John 14:2–3). He was about to create a whole new nature to accommodate the environment for His glorified humanity and, in Him, for ours. This is a picture of a new human nature and a new nature as such. The risen body is different from the mortal body and eventually involves a whole new universe. God has not tired of the "old field," but it

Dr. Edwin M. Yamauchi, professor of History at Miami University in Oxford, Ohio says, "What gives a special authority to the list [of witnesses] as historical evidence is the reference to most of the five hundred brethren being still alive. St. Paul says in effect, "If you do not believe me, you can ask them"— "Easter—Myth, Hallucination, or History?" *Christianity Today*, March 29, 1974 .

must be "weeded, dug, and sown" so a new crop can exist and flourish.

The way this new nature starts to radiate has a resemblance to the habits of the old. We got Law before Gospel, John before Jesus, miracles of the new creation before the Resurrection. Two examples of these miracles are Jesus' walking on the water and the raising of Lazarus. In the walking on the water we see nature so changed that spirit can make it do what the spirit pleases. Of course, this spirit cannot be separated from, nor disobedient to the "Father of Spirits."

Lazarus' resurrection differs from Jesus' Resurrection. Lazarus was merely restored to life, not raised to a new mode of existence. The resuscitation of Lazarus, or simple reversal, is important though because it shows again "small and close" that Jesus will raise all men at the "general resurrection." Lewis included a discussion of the miracle of Lazarus with regard to the *status quo* or "entropy" in nature using the imagery of the Humpty Dumpty story.

The Transfiguration of Jesus is also an "anticipatory glimpse" of something yet to come. In this event, Jesus is seen talking to Moses and Elijah (Luke 9:28–36). Jesus is described as luminous, as "shining whiteness" both in Luke and in His appearance in the beginning of the book of Revelation. Lewis remarked that this seems, "taken by itself" like a "vision" and that we don't know the feature of the new creation to which this event points, though he gave three possibilities.

We can know little about the new nature. "It is useful to remember that even now senses responsive to different vibrations would admit us to quite new worlds of experience: that a

Immanuel Kant (1724–1804), a German philosopher who set out to unite rationalism and empiricism. He said that all knowledge comes from sense experience but its structure is derived from the categories of the understanding, which are forms in the mind itself. His most famous works were the *Critique of Pure Reason, Critique of Practical Reason, and Critique of Judgment.* Kant distinguished between the phenomena, appearance, and noumena, things that are Real. Experience can never disclose the thing in itself. Our total experience is of the phenomenal. He took for granted that appearance implies reality. Kant could not merge the nineteenth-century scientific world, mechanistic in nature, with a world of spiritual value, freedom, moral value, the immortal soul, and God. Mechanism and freedom will never meet. Yet Kant thought that they do meet somehow mysteriously in man.

multi-dimensional space would be different, almost beyond recognition, from the space we are now aware of, yet not discontinuous from it." Such fancies "teach us not to limit, in our rashness, the vigour and variety of the new crops which this old field might yet produce." But not all that we are told of the new creation is metaphorical. The Resurrection "jerks us back"; the eating, touching, corporeal body is either reality or sheer illusion. The new nature is in the most troublesome way, interlocked in some ways with the old.

Kant is the root of a philosophical preconception from which we all suffer that makes "profoundly shocking" the idea of a new nature beyond nature, a "supernatural" existence in relation to our "five present senses," but which is "natural" from its own viewpoint. This philosophical preconception can be stated by saying that we are prepared to believe in a one-floor reality (like naturalists) or in a two-floor reality (as religion conceives it), but not in one with several floors, a skyscraper. This is the reason many believe in God but not in a world of angels, in immortality but not in the resurrection of the body, why Pantheism is popular, and why many want a Christianity without miracles (like Thomas Jefferson). Lewis himself once passionately defended this prejudice.

It is difficult to see the basis for the dogma that reality must have only two levels. There cannot be evidence that God hasn't or won't create more than one system. Nevertheless the substance of Christian teaching is that we are actually living in an even more complex situation. The new nature being created is not merely being made but recreated out of the old one. Accepting the Christian idea of intermediate floors doesn't mean we lose our "spiritual apprehension of the top floor." There is still an "undimensioned depth" where the ultimate fact, the divine life is to be found. "Most certainly also, to be united with that Life in the eternal Sonship of Christ is, strictly speaking, the only thing worth a moment's consideration."

What troubles us is not merely the statements in the text of the New Testament regarding the Ascension, for example, but what the author meant by them. Granted there are different natures, levels of being, and Christ withdrew from one to another as the first step in His creation of another. Lewis talked about the "wording" of the Ascension account in Scripture in an attempt to point to its meaning. Movement away from the moving Earth will certainly be to us movement "upwards." To say that Christ's passage to a new nature could involve no such movement, or no movement at all, within the nature he was leaving, is arbitrary. It is even more arbitrary to assume that Christ was moving in a three-dimensional space.

What does heaven mean to you? Does this view square with your best interpretation as presented in Scripture? Lewis?

But what people are actually worried about is the conviction that, whatever we say, the New Testament writers might have meant something different. Lewis addressed different understandings of the word *heaven* in this chapter: (1) the unconditioned divine life beyond all worlds, (2) blessed participation in that life by a created spirit, (3) the whole nature or system of conditions in which redeemed human spirits, still remaining human, can enjoy such participation fully and forever, the heaven Christ went to prepare for us, (4) the physical heaven, the sky, the space in which Earth moves. These distinctions are possible because of centuries of logical analysis, because we are sons of Aristotle.

Possibly every Christian alive has difficulty reconciling two things said of heaven. Heaven is said to be, first, life in Christ, a vision of God, a ceaseless adoration, and, second, a bodily life. The tension comes in that the nearer we are to the vision of God the more the body seems almost irrelevant. This discrepancy is a disorder the new creation comes to heal. We cannot do anything yet to imagine the complete healing of spirit and nature. It is presently beyond our conception. We have some faint hints perhaps (in the sacraments, in the sensuous imagery by the great poets, in the "best instances" of sexual love, in experiences of the earth's beauty).

Scripture forbids us to suppose there will be a sexual life in the new creation. This diminishes our imagination to the "withering alternative" of bodies hardly recognizable as human at all or else of a "perpetual fast." The problem is that we don't know real life in heaven. We know sex, but not the "other thing" which leaves no room for it in heaven. Where we can anticipate fullness, we anticipate fasting. The lack of a sexual life doesn't, of necessity, mean that the distinction between the sexes will disappear. No longer needed for biological purposes, the distinctions between sexes may survive for splendor.

"Heaven is a state of mind," or "spirit," is what every great religion *except* Christianity would say. Christianity teaches that God made the world, called it good, and that therefore nature cannot be "simply irrelevant" to spiritual bliss. In teaching the resurrection of the body, Christianity teaches that Heaven is not just a state of the spirit. The desire, as in the Apostle Paul, is to be reclothed, not to be unclothed.

Does all this matter? "Do not such ideas only excite us and distract us from the more immediate and more certain things, the love of God and our neighbours, the bearing of the daily cross?" If they distract you, don't think about them. It is more important to live life now. These things are written not because they're most important but because the book is about miracles. However, Lewis wouldn't admit that the things he has been discussing in the last few pages are of no importance to living the Christian life. The fact that they may be considered unimportant may account for the reason the specifically Christian virtue of hope has "grown so languid," so weak, faint, sluggish.

Christians of all people "must not conceive spiritual joy and worth as things that need to be rescued or tenderly protected from time and place and matter and the senses. Their God is the God of corn and oil and wine. He is the glad Creator. . . . To shrink back from all that can be called Nature into negative spirituality is as if we ran away from horses instead of learning to ride." There is abundant room in this pilgrim life for abstinence, renunciation, and mortifying our natural desires. But behind all asceticism should be the thought: "'Who will trust us with the true wealth if we cannot be trusted even with the wealth that perishes?' Who will trust me with a spiritual body if I cannot control even an earthly body?" As ponies are given to schoolboys, our "small and perishable bodies" have been given to us so that we should learn to manage them. We must learn to "gallop with the King" who has retained His own charger, and we should accompany Him.

The great Puritan pastor, Richard Baxter, was seldom pain free from the time he was 21 years old. At 35, he became gravely ill and expected to die. In preparation for his death, Baxter meditated on the joys of heaven and wrote his reflections in a book, *The Saints' Everlasting Rest.* Baxter recovered from his illness and lived forty-one more years. "Baxter's meditation filled him with joy and proved to be a source of seemingly boundless energy!...[Baxter] would argue that it is only when persons are heavenly-minded that they can be of any earthly good. Focused meditation upon heaven will supply believer with energy and direction for living in the present"—Timothy K. Beougher in a Preface to *The Saints' Everlasting Rest,* The Billy Graham Center, Wheaton, Illinois, 1994, 10.

# ℵ COMMENTARY

The Resurrection of Jesus Christ is the most important doctrine of the Christian faith. It is as *essential* as theology and as history! Christians since the New Testament have argued for the centrality of the doctrine, convinced that it proved Jesus' deity and the efficacy of His death for our sins. Paul, for example, considered the Resurrection to be the cornerstone of the Christian faith: If Jesus did not rise from the dead, the whole structure of Christianity collapses.

The Christian faith, and its claim to be truth, exists only if Jesus rose from the dead, because the heart of Christianity is a living Christ (see Phil. 3:20–21; 2 Cor. 5:1–5; 1 Thess. 4:16–17).

The fact that Jesus rose bodily (in a real physical body) from the grave has been fundamental to Christian teaching from the beginning. In the New Testament Jesus' appearance is depicted as spiritual—in the sense of being independent of the ordinary laws of nature—but also as material or physical. He invited followers to touch His hands and feet, for a spirit does not have "flesh and bones" (Luke 24:39–40; see also Matt. 27:61–66; 28:1–20; Mark 16:1–20; Luke 24:1–53; John 20:10–31).

## CHAPTER 17: EPILOGUE

Lewis's work has ended. You should now turn to a study of the historical evidence yourself beginning with the New Testament, not with books *about* the New Testament. He suggested that if you don't know Greek you should get a modern translation. Then, when you turn from the New Testament itself to modern scholars,

"And if Christ has not been raised, our preaching is useless and so is your faith. More than that, we are then found to be false witnesses about God. . . . And if Christ has not been raised, your faith is futile" (1 Cor. 15:14, 17).

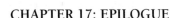

Why is the bodily Resurrection of Jesus so important to the Christian faith?

Lewis cautioned you to remember that "you go among them as a sheep among wolves." Truer words were never spoken! "Naturalistic assumptions, beggings of the question such as that which I noted on the first page of this book, will meet you on every side—even from the pens of clergymen." This is because we all have the "hangover" of naturalism in our bones. Here is a serious warning to be careful what secondary sources you use. Be forewarned!

The Epilogue ends by giving two final warnings regarding monism, naturalism, what he calls "*Everythingism,*" or the state of mind that says that "miracles don't happen." First, you must expect a "counter-attack" by nature. "The moment rational thought ceases, imagination, mental habit, temperament, and the 'spirit of the age' take charge of you again. New thoughts, until they have themselves become habitual, will affect your consciousness as a whole only while you are actually thinking them." Yes, counterarguments against miracles must be given "full attention," but you must also be careful that the mind is not simply gravitating back to its habitual outlook. A "psychology of disbelief" is hard to shake even when in the light of fact, evidence, history, and reason on the side of Christianity.

Second, you are probably right that you will never see a miracle and are probably equally correct in thinking that there was a natural explanation for anything which happened in your life. "God does not shake miracles into Nature at random as if from a pepper-caster. They come on great occasions: they are found at the great ganglions of history—not of political or social history, but of that spiritual history which cannot be fully known by men." Unless

Lewis said that God is, perhaps, trying a grand new experiment wherein all believers are expected to become "sages." This hits right at the heart of the doctrine of the priesthood of all believers. Why is this important? How does it impact you, especially in light of Lewis's warning here?

your life is near one of these "great ganglions," you shouldn't expect to see a miracle. The analogy is given: If you don't live near a railway, you shouldn't expect to see trains going past your windows. "That we should see a miracle is even less likely. Nor, if we understand, shall we be anxious to do so. 'Nothing almost sees miracles but misery.' Miracles and martyrdoms tend to bunch about the same areas of history—areas we have naturally no wish to frequent."

## APPENDIX A: ON THE WORDS "SPIRIT" AND "SPIRITUAL"

The kind of analysis made of any complex thing depends on the purpose in view. The angle from which man is approached in chapter 4 is different from the way that would be proper in a devotional or practical essay on the spiritual life. Lewis listed the ways the words *spirit, spirits,* and *spiritual* are, or have been, used in English: a chemical sense, a now obsolete medical sense, simply the opposite of the body or material, the supernatural element given to every man at his creation (the rational element), the Christian sense which means the life arising when we voluntarily surrender to divine grace and become children of God in Christ.

In the New Testament, the maturity of a Christian is not judged by the "gifts of the Spirit" but by the "fruit of the Spirit" (Gal. 5:22–23). Discuss some of the similarities and differences between unregenerate and regenerate man.

We must be careful that our words do not change their meaning during discussion. It might be helpful to give different names for what is meant by the word *spirit.*

Lewis included a short discussion of the sameness and difference between unregenerate and regenerate man.

## APPENDIX B: ON "SPECIAL PROVIDENCES"

Many devout people speak of certain happenings as being "providential' or "special providences" but don't mean by this that they were miracles. The example is given of the weather that allowed the British to save their army at Dunkirk. Some viewed this weather as "providential." "The Christian doctrine that some events, though not miracles, are yet answers to prayer, would seem at first to imply this."

However, Lewis could not envision an intervening class of events that are neither miraculous nor ordinary. "Either the weather at Dunkirk was or was not that which the previous physical history of the universe, by its own character, would inevitably produce. If it was, then how is it 'specially' providential? If it was not, then it was a miracle." The idea that there is a special class of events, other than miracles, that can be distinguished as "specially providential" must be abandoned.

Sometimes to get any picture of a thing at all, it is necessary to start with a false picture and make the needed corrections. Lewis started with the false picture of providence and used a lengthy analogy of the novelist. However, we created beings have free will, and at this juncture the false picture of providence must begin to be corrected. The picture of providence that had been used "was false because it represented God and Nature as inhabiting a common Time. But it is probably that Nature is not really in Time and almost certain that God is not. Time is probably (like perspective) the mode of our perception." Lewis mentioned Thomas Aquinas' doctrine of foreknowledge and the "eternal Now." "In this sense God did not create the

*Foreknowledge*—The teaching that God knows everything that will occur in the future of the universe. Because God is not a part of the space/time continuum, He can know what human beings will experience as future in a way that does not destroy human freedom. How God experiences time is similar (analogous) to how human beings experience it: Just as it is always now for us (we experience the past only in our memories, and the future only in our hopes), thus God sees everything in one eternal now, or present. What He knows as present, we experience as past, present, and future. Jesus seemed to have this foreknowledge even during His Incarnation (Matt. 24:35–44; Mark 9:1ff; Luke 12:40, 21:20ff.)—Miethe, *The Compact Dictionary.*

universe long ago but creates it at this minute—at every minute."

Lewis attempted to explain free will by exploring an analogy involving a piece of paper on which a black wavy line is already drawn. The black line represents a creature with free will, red lines added later represent material events, and the "I" in the story represents God. The model would be more accurate if God made the paper and there were hundreds of millions of black lines on the paper.

All this is related to the concept of prayer. Most of our prayers fit two categories. We ask for (1) a miracle or (2) events the ground of which would have to have been laid when the universe began. "But then to God (though not to me) I and the prayer I make in 1945 were just as much present at the creation of the world as they are now and will be a million years hence. God's creative act is timeless and timelessly adapted to the "free" elements within it: but this timeless adaptation meets our consciousness as a sequence and a prayer and answer."

From this "two corollaries" follow: (1) Was a given event, though not a miracle, an answer to prayer? All events in the real world, with the exception of miracles, happen as a result of natural causes. "Providence" and natural causes both determine every event because they are one, not alternatives. (2) When we are praying, say for a battle or a medical problem, the event has already been decided. But this is not a reason to stop praying. "The event certainly has been decided—in a sense it was decided 'before all worlds.' But one of the things taken into account in deciding it, and therefore one of the things that really cause it to happen, may be this very prayer that we are now offering." Free acts contribute to the cosmic shape.

A final consequence remains. It cannot be proven empirically that a particular, nonmiraculous event was or was not answered prayer. Because the event was not miraculous, the skeptic can always point to a natural cause. The validity of prayer has to be asserted or denied with regard to an act of will which chooses or rejects faith in light of a whole philosophy, a worldview. The impossibility of empirical proof is a spiritual necessity.

It is not important for the Christian to ask if this or that event was the result of prayer. Rather he or she is "to believe that all events without exception are *answers* to prayer in the sense that whether they are grantings or refusals the prayers of all concerned and their needs have all been taken into account." God hears all prayers but doesn't say yes to all. Lewis believed that if an event happens for which you have prayed, then your prayer has always added to it. When the opposite happens, your prayer has been heard and refused "for your ultimate good and the good of the whole universe." We will always deceive ourselves by trying to find special evidence that some particular act or event was an answer to prayer more than other events if a miracle was not involved.

"It may be a mystery why He should have allowed us to cause real events at all; but it is no odder that He should allow us to cause them by praying than by any other method"—C. S. Lewis, *Letters to Malcolm:Chiefly on Prayer.* Harcourt Brace Jovanovich.

Barratt, David. *C. S. Lewis and His World*. Grand Rapids: Eerdmans, 1987.

Christensen, Michael. *C. S. Lewis on Scripture*. Waco, Tex.: Word, 1979; London: Hodder, 1980.

Christopher, Joe R., and Joan K. Ostling. *C. S. Lewis: An Annotated Checklist of Writings about Him and His Works*. Kent, Ohio: Kent State University Press, 1974.

Como, James T. (ed.). *C. S. Lewis at the Breakfast Table: And Other Reminiscences*. New York: Macmillan, 1979.

Cunningham, Richard B. *C. S. Lewis: Defender of the Faith*. Philadelphia: Westminster Press, 1967.

Gibson, Evan. *C. S. Lewis, Spinner of Tales*. Grand Rapids: Eerdmans, 1980.

Gilbert, Douglas and Clyde Kilby. *C. S. Lewis: Images of His World*. Grand Rapids: Eerdmans, 1973.

Gresham, Douglas H. *Lenten Lands: My Childhood with Joy Davidman and C. S. Lewis*. New York: Macmillan, 1988.

Howard, Thomas. *The Achievement of C. S. Lewis*. Wheaton, Ill.: Harold Shaw, 1980.

Keefe, Carolyn. *C. S. Lewis: Speaker and Teacher*. Grand Rapids: Zondervan, 1971.

Kilby, Clyde. *Images of Salvation in the Fiction of C. S. Lewis*. Wheaton, Ill.: Harold Shaw, 1978.

_____. *The Christian World of C. S. Lewis*. Grand Rapids: Eerdmans, 1964.

Kreeft, Peter. *C. S. Lewis: A Critical Essay*. Grand Rapids: Eerdmans, 1969.

Lindskoog, Kathryn. *The C. S. Lewis Hoax*. Portland, Ore.: Multnomah Press, 1988.

Miethe, Terry. *The Compact Dictionary of Doctrinal Terms*. Minneapolis, Minn.: Bethany House Publishers, 1988.

Peters, John. *C. S. Lewis: The Man and His Achievement*. London: Paternoster, 1985.

Purtill, Richard. *Lord of the Elves and Eldils: Fantasy and Philosophy in C. S. Lewis and J. R. R. Tolkien*. Grand Rapids: Zondervan, 1974.

Sayer, George. *Jack: A Life of C. S. Lewis*. Wheaton, Ill.: Crossway Books, 1994.

Schakel, Peter Jr. (ed.). *The Longing for a Form: Essays on the Fiction of C. S. Lewis*. Kent, Ohio: Kent State University Press, 1977.

Sibley, Brian. *Shadowlands*. London: Hodder & Stoughton, 1985.

Walsh, Chad. *C. S. Lewis: Apostle to the Skeptics*. New York: Macmillan, 1949; Folcraft, Penn.: Folcraft Library Editions, 1974.

_____. *The Literary Legacy of C. S. Lewis*. New York: Harcourt Brace Jovanovich, 1980.

Willis, John Randoph, S. J. *Pleasures Forever: The Theology of C. S. Lewis*.

SHEPHERD'S NOTES

# SHEPHERD'S NOTES

_____

_____

_____

_____

_____

_____

_____

_____

_____

_____

_____

_____

_____

_____

_____

_____

_____

_____

_____

# SHEPHERD'S NOTES